JOANNA JANIK

TERMS OF THE SEMANTIC SPHERE
OF δίκη AND θέμις
IN THE EARLY GREEK EPIC

POLSKA AKADEMIA UMIEJĘTNOŚCI

PRACE KOMISJI
FILOLOGII KLASYCZNEJ

Nr 30

POD REDAKCJĄ
ROMUALDA TURASIEWICZA

KRAKÓW 2003

POLISH ACADEMY OF ARTS AND SCIENCES

STUDIES OF THE COMMISSION ON CLASSICAL PHILOLOGY
VOL. 30

JOANNA JANIK

TERMS OF THE SEMANTIC SPHERE
OF δίκη AND θέμις
IN THE EARLY GREEK EPIC

KRAKÓW 2003

Publication financed by the Committee for Scientific Research

Editor of the series
Romuald Turasiewicz

Executive editors:
Elżbieta Fiałek
Zdzisław J. Kapera

ISBN 83-88857-54-1
ISSN 0079-3272

Distributed by
Polska Akademia Umiejętności, ul. Sławkowska 17
31-016 Kraków, Poland, tel./fax: (48 12) 422-54-22
e-mail: office@pau.krakow.pl

and by
The Enigma Press, ul. Podedworze 5,
32-031 Mogilany, Poland, tel. (48 12) 270-08-70
e-mail: zjkapera@vela.filg.uj.edu.pl

Printed by
"Ekodruk", Kraków

CONTENTS

Introduction

The aim of this study is to analyse of the history of θέμις and δίκη in the early Greek literature, i. e., Homer and Hesiod. The subject has been discussed for a very long time and our survey is supposed to continue the debate. The interpretation of a term is always difficult and it is especially so when the sources are of strictly literary character. Works of literature are not supposed to define abstract notions, neither are they expected to describe in detail the ways in which the concrete terms were used by the contemporary people. What we should do is to read the works preserved up to the present day and try to understand the mentality of the past. The variety of interpretations and the differences between various editions of the texts prove that it is not an easy task.

Our study is based on the analysis of almost all passages where the terms δίκη, θέμις and their derivatives appear. The aim of this procedure is to demonstrate the development of the abstract ideas of justice and order which, in the following centuries, will stand in the centre of Greek ethical thought. These terms are of particular interest because of their significance for the concept of a state and a society. Θέμις as well as δίκη denoted norms, then laws and, eventually, the principle of justice, which ruled the human community and made social life possible.

The main part of this work is devoted to Homer, since the variety of senses and the difficulties connected with the interpretation of Homeric text make this analysis very complicated. The analysis was based on the rich and excellent studies written, among others, by: Victor Ehernberg, Rudolf Hirzel, Hermann Fraenkel, Romuald Turasiewicz, A. W. H. Adkins, Eric A. Havelock, Bruno Snell, Adam Krokiewicz, H. Wolf, Hildebrecht Hommel and many other eminent scholars. For the questions of the language and style, we used the works of Milman Parry (in the "New Companion to Homer", ed. by Morris and Powell, Leiden-New York-Köhln 1997) and Kazimierz Korus. While discussing the history of the state and society we turned to the studies of Victor Ehrenberg, Donald Kagan, M. I. Finley, Kurt A. Raaflaub, Klaus Rosen and many others. The history of Greek law was based mainly on the works of Michael Gagarin, J. W. Jones and Gerhard Thür.

The interpretation of Hesiod seems to be more coherent and consistent. However, also in the poetry of Hesiod there are passages the meaning of which remains obscure.

The main point of reference was the commentary provided by Martin L. West.

The world of Homeric epics

Whoever wants to analyse evolution of any term important in Greek culture, even less crucial than δίκη, always begins his study with the "Iliad" and the "Odyssey". These two epics are not only the beginning of Greek literature. They have also been regarded as the most important books, the role of which goes far beyond pleasure and relaxation given by a well-written story. In the antiquity, the Homeric masterpiece was supposed to teach. There are reasons to believe that its didactic function sometimes overshadowed its literary perfection.[1] Generations of Greeks sought in Homer inspiration and guidance. Together with Hesiod, Homer played the role of a great Hellenic teacher, a source of knowledge covering aesthetics, morals, religion, social conduct and some technical advice regarding, for example, military tactic.[2] What makes the "Iliad" and the "Odyssey" so unique is the fact that they have never been replaced by any other work. The Greek society was changed, the process of its development was slower or quicker, but not interrupted, and the Homeric poems remained the Greek Bible for all that time. They were admired, accepted without a moment of hesitation or objected and criticised[3], but for Greek moralists, philosophers and the so called ordinary men in the street they remained terms of reference.[4] In his study on the Greek concept of justice, E.A. Havelock stresses this aspect of Homeric epics.[5] At this point one should ask a question about the time when these poems were composed. That question cannot be answered with a great deal of accuracy. The same regards the author. Differences in language, style and the world depicted in both poems let us assume that the "Iliad" was composed earlier than the "Odyssey", either as a whole or as a series of songs, united later by a talented poet.[6] We will also accept a vast space of time when they were

---

[1] E. A. H a v e l o c k, *The Greek Concept of Justice*, Cambridge, Mass. 1978, p. 5.

[2] *Ibidem*, p. 7.

[3] *Ibidem*, *l.cit.*

[4] For the analysis of some particular aspects of Homeric style, see: K. K o r u s, *Die Griechiesche Satire, Die Theoretischen grundlagen und Ihre Anwendung auf Homer Epic,* Warszawa-Kraków 1991; the importance of Homer for the development of the philosophy was underlined by F. M. Cornford, who draws the line going from the seer through the poet stright to the philosopher, see: F. M. C o r n f o r d, *Principium Sapientiae. A Study of the Origins of Greek Philosophical Thought,* New York 1965, pp. 79-80, 107-127.

[5] E. A. H a v e l o c k, *op.cit.*, pp. 4-15.

[6] For the complex analysis, see; R. T u r a s i e w i c z, *Homer,* Kraków 1971, J. L a t a c z, *Homer. Der erste Dichter des Abendlnds,* München-Zürich 1989, F. M. T u r n e r, *The*

composed: the 8th century B.C.[7] The identity of the author, or authors, is not of much importance for this study. Therefore, no matter how interesting this issue seems to be, we are allowed to leave it out. The problem of primary importance for anyone examining the development of a term connected with the social and political evolution of hellenic society, is the question concerning the world presented in the "Iliad" and the "Odyssey". Does Homer describe the world of Golden Mycenae bygone in his time or does he speak of his own reality, sometimes disguised in the costume of the past, which is supposed to make it more attractive for the listeners? Did the world of Achilles and Odysseus really exist or are we dealing with poetic creation? The authority of well-known specialists[8] in the field lets us assume that the answer lays somewhere between these statements.[9] The world created by the poet partly adheres to the former period: traces of the bygone Mycenaean civilization were probably preserved in the formulae that could have been transmitted from one generation to another and, finally, inherited by Homer.[10] The poet apparently intended to depict the "old time", but his knowledge was too limited to carry out this task. For example, Greek and Trojan knights ride chariots, but they use them just as a mere means of transport. We may suspect that Homer did not know whether they could play any other role in a battle; in his own time this weapon was probably not too popular. Homeric *basileis* and *wanaktes* resemble Mycenaean terms, but they are used differently[11]: in Mycenae *wanaks* was the title of the highest ruler, whereas the

---

Homeric Question, [in:] *A New Companion to Homer,* ed. by I. Morris and P. Powell, London-New York-Köln 1997, pp. 123-145.

[7] J. Latacz in his thorough analysis suggests the second half of the 8th century; see: J. L a t a c z, *op.cit.,* pp. 77-90.

[8] M. I. F i n l e y, *The World of Odysseus,* New York 1954, p. 11, D. K a g a n, *History of Greek Political Thought,* New York 1965, pp. 2-14, and one of the most recent works: K. R a a f l a u b, *Homeric Society,* in: *A New Companion to Homer,* ed. by I. Morris and P. Powell, London-New York- Köln 1997, 625 ff. According to M. I. Finley, the world of Homeric epics is generally post-Mycenaean and the break between the two periods is deep and permanent. In the opinion of K. Raaflaub, the dating of Homeric society should be based on the tradition and character of the epic oral poetry which should be "historical in appearance but contemporary in meaning". When we consider the poet's effort to preserve "epic distance", we may assume that Homeric society is near-contemporary with the poet, i. e. of the late ninth and eighth centuries (K. Raaflaub follows the opinion that the epics were composed in the second half of the eighth century, the "Iliad" about one generation before the "Odyssey").

[9] The resent results can be found in *A New Companion to Homer,* ed. Morris and Powell, Leiden-New York-Köln 1997; especially see: J. B e n n e t, *Homer and the Bronze Age, ibidem,* pp. 511-533. I. M o r r i s, *Homer and the Iron Age, ibidem,* pp. 534-559.

[10] D. Kegan, *op.cit.,* pp. 2-14.

[11] *Ibidem*; to compare with: E. B e n v e n i s t e, *Le Vocabulaire des institutions indo-*

basileis had an inferior rank; in the "Iliad" and the "Odyssey" only the most important kings have the right to be called *basileis* and the term *wanax* is used much more often. In Homeric world, there is no trace of the complicated bureaucracy that ruled the domain of Mycenaean master. The first glance at the preserved Minoan paintings and figures assures us that Homeric heros and heroines do not look like people living in the time of Trojan war (around 1200 B.C.). These and many other facts make us believe that Homer does not describe the historical past; neither does he depict his own time; the world of Achilles and Odysseus is a poetic fiction in the sense that it has never existed. However, this fantastic world has, in our opinion, some more realistic aspects, namely the ideas, which express the mentality of people living in the 9th or the beginning of the 8th century B.C. They also reflect, at least partly, the level of social development. In this period, the Greek polis came into existence and these two magnificent epic poems are the most complete source to study the process of its creation.

Some scholars claim that in the "Iliad" there is no polis at all, and this term can be referred only to the later "Odyssey", or even locate the Homeric society in the pre-polis period.[12] However, this statement seems to be too categorical. The action in the "Iliad" takes place in Troy and the surrounding area; a limited space with two important points: the city of Priam and the Achaean military camp. Homer uses three words for a city: πόλις, ἄστυ,

---

européennes, Paris 1969, vol. II, pp. 23 ff; the term *wanaks* denotes the real political power, whereas *basileus* (the etymology of this word remains uncertain and cannot be of any help) seems to be a traditional title, which is not necessarily connected with territorial authority. According to E. Benveniste in the past the term *basileus* never denoted a king, rather a local ruler; *wanaks* was reserved to the king and used to be applied to describe the gods. On the other hand, Aristotle observed that the relation between *basileus* and *wanaks* corresponded to the connection between a king and a prince. However, the notion of *basileus* in Homer describes a ruler who has a real power and his position is based even more on the authority than on any defined rule. His authority comes from Zeus (although the highest god has never been called *basileus*). The visible symbol of this power is the sceptre, σκῆπτρον. The divine protection does not mean the divinity of the king himself. Moreover, E. Benveniste emphasizes the difference between Greek concept of kingship and other Indo-European ideas of royal power. The Greeks have developed a more democratic and, in our terms, more modern notion.

N. Y a m a g a t a (see: Aναξ and βασιλεύς in Homer, Classical Quartarly 47 (1997), pp. 1-14) underlines that βασιλεύς is always describing humans and never gods (unlike ἄναξ) and that this term denotes position connected with certain privileges and donations. Therefore, the term can be used in different grades (βασιλεύτερος, βασιλεύτατος) corresponding to the rank and prestige of the man described with this word.

[12] V. E h r e n b e r g (*Polis und Imperium,* ed. by K. F. Stroheker and A. J. Graham, Zurich 1965, p. 93) claims that this structure can be seen only in the later poem, M. I. F i n l e y believes that in the Homeric epics *polis* has not emerged yet (*op.cit.,* p. 156).

πτολίεθρον, the meaning of which remains rather obscure. The first term dominates. Troy is called πόλις and this use is not restricted to the meaning of the former πτόλις: it defines not only the citadel, the upper part of the city, but also the rest of it. (Earlier, the lower part of the city was called ἄστυ). In Homer, there are little differences between these two terms.[13] They are used almost interchangeably. It is also worth mentioning that in Homer there is no word for a village and, as a matter of fact, there is no village.[14] People generally live in cities, which seem to be the most basic social organisms, consisting of a town (walls, houses, temples, streets, agoras) and a human community ruled by a certain order. Certainly, the abstract meaning of the word *polis*, connected with *politeia*, is not always what Homeric men have in mind when they use it. But sometimes we have an impression of such use; for example, when Glaukos says to Hector: "Consider now how you may save the *polis* and the *astu*"[15] - the state and the city. In any case, no matter with what level of abstraction do we deal in this line, we should stress that Homeric society, even that described in the "Iliad", lives in πόλεις, which constitutes the most important social and political structure. We may also add that the Greek military camp with its buildings, walls, the place for meetings corresponding to an *agora*, resembles a town. In the "Odyssey", the situation is much simpler, we have a chance to see many πόλεις and to look at the life of its citizens. Provided that we do not identify πόλις with the democratic πόλις, there is no doubt that in Homer we are able to see the first form of this structure.[16]

No human community is able to survive without rules that keep it together and make life in such a community possible. In Greek culture we have many terms denoting these phenomena, e.g. θέμις, νόμος, δίκη, εὐνομία, all of them associated with the sense of justice, law and order. We are convinced that the history of a πόλις must have been parallel to the development of these terms, especially δίκη. When speaking about the development of a term's meaning we do not imply that it is equal to the process of conscious abstracting of the idea of justice, since we assume that people can use an idea, comprehend its meaning and take it into consideration without being able to formulate its definition. People generally use some basic concepts and claim to under-

[13] S. S c u l l y, *Homer and the sacred city*, Ithaca – London 1990, pp. 6-16.

[14] W. H o f f m a n n, *Die Polis bei Homer*, [in:] *Zur griechischen Staatskunde*, hrsg. von F. Gschnitzer, Darmstadt 1969, pp. 123-138.

[15] S. S c u l l y, *op.cit.*, pp. 8-9, Iliad, 17, 144.

[16] The same view is presented by K. R a a f l a u b (*op. cit.*, p. 645) who locates the Homeric society in the period of early *polis*. He emphasizes the significance of well-established communal structures, like the assembly and the council.

stand them, although they would not answer any Socratic question beginning with: "What is X?". As some scholars claim, cultural information is encoded and transmitted from generation to generation in the language.[17] This cultural storage becomes the foundation of our social identity. In case of oral culture or nonliteracy of the society, the ways of preserving and spreading cultural information are restricted to few forms. It may seem extremely difficult to understand how this process is possible without any sort of visible artefacts. In the history of Greek culture, the period known as "Dark Ages" can be used as the illustration of this phenomenon. There can be little doubt that it was epic poetry that became the most important way of expressing the concepts and ideas, which were the fundamental elements of Greek identity. Poetry is not philosophy and it would be false to look for compound definitions of abstract terms in the "Iliad" or the "Odyssey". Nevertheless, there are many authors whose disappointment caused by that simple fact can hardly be covered by their admiration for Homer's masterpiece. In Greek literature till the beginning of philosophy *sensu stricto* we find only a description, not a definition. We are able to see what justice means, how just people behave, what sort of deeds deserve the adjective "just", but we will not find any sentence explaining what exactly justice is. The limited use of the verb "to be" is connected with the form of composition.[18]

---

[17] H a v e l o c k, *op.cit.*, pp. 9-11.
[18] *Ibidem.*

Δίκη in the "Iliad"

According to E.A.Havelock[1], one of the most important terms and its derivatives denoting, in the "Iliad", the legal principle of the life of human community, occurs in the text about 12 times. The terms of primary importance are: δίκη[2], δικάζειν, δικάζεσθαι, δικασπόλοι, δίκαιος (δικαιότατος). In several places in the "Odyssey", δίκη together with genitive case means: the way of, characteristic of; it always refers to a group, never to an individual.[3] However, in that meaning it does not occur in the "Iliad", where the meaning of δίκη is usually connected in the same way with legal procedure. The association with modern terms seems to be natural, but in the Homeric epics, the meaning of the so called "legal procedure" is far from being clear and easy to translate. We use the expression "so called", because even the existence of legal procedure in Homer is doubtful and in the abundant literature referring to the subject[4], there is no unanimity. There

---

[1] E. A. H a v e l o c k, *The Greek Concept of Justice,* Cambridge, Mass. 1978, pp. 9-11.

[2] The ethymology of δίκη is not clear; see: P. C h a n t r a i n e, *Dictionnaire éthymologique de la langue grecque,* Paris 1990. Two possible roots are taken into consideration: δικ- and δεικ-. E. B e n v e n i s t e (*op.cit.*, vol. II, pp. 108 ff) claims that δίκη comes from δεικ-, but he also discusses the problems connected with such ethymology. δείκνυμι (δεικ-) means "to show", therefore there is no direct transition from this word to the term δίκη. The meaning:"to show, to demonstrate" is not clear; does it mean "to point with a finger", or "to show with words" (this possibility is much more probable)? And what sort of showing is it? demonstrating something as an example? The logical explanation is that the primary sense of δίκη was "to show what should be done, i. e. to define the norm". The same: H. H o m m e l, *Die Gerichtsszene auf dem Schild des Achilleus; zur Pflege des Rechts in Homerischen Zeit,* Symbolae B. II, Hildesheim-Zürich-New York 1988, pp. 46-82 V. E h r e n b e r g (*Die rechtsidee im frühen Griechentum,* Leipzig 1921, pp. 70-71) claims that δίκη comes from δικεῖν "to throw", so δίκη is "der Wurf", "a throw", and this meaning helps to understand the expressions ἰθεῖα or σκολιὰ δίκη and ἐς μέσον δικάζειν., see also: O. F l ü g e l, *Die Idee des Rechts und Gerechtigkeit bei Homer und Hesiod,* Pädagogisches Magazin, Heft 360, Beyer und Mann, 1909.

[3] M. G a g a r i n, *Dike in the Work and Days",* Classical Philology 68 (1973), pp. 81-94; *Dike in Archaic Greek Thought,* Classical Philology 69 (1974), pp. 186-97.

[4] The most important books: E. W o l f, *Griechischen Rechtsdenken,*Frankfurt am Main 1950, U. Wesel, *Geschichte des Rechts von Frühformen bis zum Vertrag von Maastricht,*München 1997, G. T h ü r, *Oaths and the Dispute Settlement in Ancient Greek Law,* in: *Greek Law in Its Political Settings,* ed. by L. Foxhall and A. D. E. Lewis, Oxford 1996, pp. 57-72, K. L a t t e, *Der Rechtsgedanke in archaischen Griechentum,* Antike und

are a few basic questions the answers to which are crucial when one tries to understand the scenes of disputes. The first and the most important question is whether we can speak about any legal procedure and about any law in Homer at all? Is the society shown in Homer developed enough to have law? And if the answer is positive, how can the law, which has not been written yet, act? L. Gernet defines the "pre-law", i. e. the stage of development prior to the law characterised as a procedure supported by a social organisation of judgement.[5] In order to build his concept of pre-law, he examines the evidence from myth and cult coming from the oldest time, older even than the epic poetry. In recent years, this theory was partly followed by M. Gagarin, who presented a highly interesting conception of three-stage development of human society.[6] However, it should be stressed that this theory was based on the very restrictive definition of law[7] defined as a formal, abstract set of rules accepted by the authorities and enacted in the form of a written code. According to this definition, the society described by Homer does not have laws. It seems to be on the first stage of legal evolution, i. e. in the period when the disputes are settled publicly and by a voluntary consent of the litigants. The next stage brings the enforcement of settlements, the final stage begins when people are obliged to respect written rules and settle their disputes in front of the tribunal.

In his *"Geschichte des Rechts"*, U. Wesel underlines the evolutionary character of law.[8] The law changed its functions: in the beginning it was strongly connected with religion and almost identified with morals. Before

---

Abendland B. II (1946), pp. 63-76, J. W. J o n e s, *The Law and the Legal Theory of the Greeks*, Aalen 1977, H. H o m m e l, *Die Gerichtsszene auf dem Schild des Achilleus; zur Pflege des Rechts in Homerischen Zeit*, Symbolae B. II, Hildesheim - Zürich - New York 1988, pp. 46-82, S. C. H u m p h r e y s, *Anthropology and the Greeks*, London 1978, L. G e r n e t, *The Anthropology of Ancient Greece*, London 1981, M. G a g a r i n, *Early Greek Law*, Berkeley-Los Angeles-London 1986, V. E h r e n b e r g, *Rechtsidee im frühen Griechentum*, Leipzig 1921, in Polish literature: P. W y g a n o w s k i, *"Dike" u Homera*, Meander 7-8 (1994), pp. 327-340.Wyganowski's analysis is interesting and gives a lecturer an interesting and coherent picture of the Homeric legal procedure and his vision of justice, although the image seems to be too easily obtained; some opinions of the author are plausible, for example the importance of the legal procedure, the role of a king, nevertheless, I cannot fully agree with the econclusion that θέμιστες in the *"Odyssey"* signify the procedural rules and the results of these procedures is δίκη. W g a n o w s k i underlines the legal meaning of δίκη which belongs to his interpretation of the *"Iliad"*.

[5] L. G e r n e t, *op.cit.*, II, pp. 107 – 111.

[6] M G a g a r i n (1986), *op.cit.*, pp. 3-11.

[7] For the thorough discussion connected with the term of prelaw see: K. J. B u r c h f i e l, *The myth of "Prelaw" in Early Greece*, Symposion 1993, pp. 79-104.

[8] U. W e s e l, *op.cit.*, pp. 45-54.

the emergence of a state, it maintained order and justice. Later law assumed one more function: it became the instrument of rule and, on the next stage, the means of control over the ruling power.

Most of the modern authors agree that in order to conduct the most exhaustive analysis of the early Greek law, one should not exclude the method of comparison. The work of legal anthropologists provides a different model of survey and makes it possible to formulate different type of questions referring to the definition of law. As K. J. Burchfiel says[9] summarizing the anthropological theories of last decades, the traditional definition of law, based on criteria more or less close to these used by M. Gagarin, is fully applicable to the Western modern law, but cannot be applied to a different cultural model. The Eurocentric theory of law also excludes all these types of social order that had been formed before the principles created during the centuries of legal development came into being. The broader definition supported by anthropological evidence lets us claim that "neither writing nor formulation of abstract systems of legal rules is a necessary prerequisite for complex system of law."[10] E. Cantarella claims that precise and distinct legal rules can be found in the epic poetry[11] while L. Gernet, having examined the evidence of myths, listed several rights, for instance: the right to avenge homicide, the right to claim an inheritance.[12]

The discussion referring to the basic question: "to what stage of Greek history are we entitled to apply the term >law<?", seems to have no definite conclusion. The opinions are divided into two groups: some scholars support the theory of "proto-legal" period in early Greek history[13], the others are trying to prove that there is no such thing as "pre-law"[14] (either because even the order depicted by Homer deserves the adjective "legal", or because there is no law whatsoever in the Homeric world).

We will not try to solve this complicated problem, since, in our opinion, the evidence provided by the Homeric epics is not sufficient to verify any of these hypotheses. On the other hand, it was necessary to present main opinions concerning that matter before we started the analysis of particular lines of the text and the meaning of the term δίκη. In our opinion, in Homer we certainly deal with the sort of procedures that can be interpreted as

---

[9] K. J. B u r c h f i e l, *op. cit.*, pp. 88-104.

[10] K. J. B u r c h f i e l, *op. cit.*, p. 89.

[11] see: K. J. B u r c h f i e l, notes 58-60, 90; E. C a n t a r e l l a, *Tra diritto e prediritto: un problema aperto,* Dialogues d'histoire 13 (1987), 149-181.

[12] L. G e r n e t, *The Anthropology of Ancient Greece,* London 1981, p. 175 ff.

[13] For example: L. Gernet, M. Gagarin.

[14] K. J. B u r c h f i e l, *op.cit.*, p. 89.

"proto-legal" in the sense that they are performed in order to settle disputes. They show the rules in action, although the exact meaning of these rules may sometimes be obscure. The procedures depicted in Homer are not "legal" in the modern sense of this term and according to modern standards there is no law in Homeric society. Nevertheless, this society had already worked up some proceedings that allowed them to solve arguments without violence, and the term δίκη was in the centre of this process.

Two passages from the "Iliad" are the most important for the analysis: the famous scene from the shield of Achilles (Il. 18. 498-510) and the argument between Menelaus and Antilochus that takes place after the horse race (Il. 23. 566-585).

The most adequate fragment comes from the book 18 (Il.18. 496-510):

λαοὶ δ' εἰν ἀγορῇ ἦσαν ἀθρόοι; ἔνθα δὲ νεῖκος
ὠρώρει, δύο δ' ἄνδρες ἐνείκεον εἵνεκα ποινῆς
ἀνδρὸς ἀποφθιμένου; ὃ μὲν εὔχετο πάντ' ἀποδοῦναι
δήμῳ πιφαύσκων, ὃ δ' ἀναίνετο μηδὲν ἑλέσθαι;
ἄμφω δ' ἰέσθην ἐπὶ ἴστορι πεῖραρ ἑλέσθαι.
Λαοὶ δ' ἀμφοτέροισιν ἐπήπυον ἀμφὶς ἀρωγοί;
κήρυκες δ' ἄρα λαὸν ἐρήτυον; οἳ δὲ γέροντες
εἵατ' ἐπὶ ξεστοῖσι λίθοις ἱερῷ ἐνὶ κύκλῳ,
σκῆπτρα δὲ κηρύκων ἐν χέρσ' ἔχον ἠεροφώνων;
τοῖσιν ἔπειτ' ἤϊσσον, ἀμοιβηδὶς δὲ δίκαζον.
κεῖτο δ' ἄρ' ἐν μέσσοισι δύω χρυσοῖο τάλαντα,
τῷ δόμεν ὃς μετὰ τοῖσι δίκην ἰθύντατα εἴποι.

But the folk were gathered in the place of assembly; for there a strife had arisen, and two men were striving about the blood-price of a man slain; the one avowed that he had paid all, declaring his cause to the people, but the other refused to accept aught; and each was fain to win the issue on the word of a daysman. Moreover, the folk were cheering both, showing favour to this side and to that. And heralds held back the folk, and the elders were sitting upon polished stones in the sacred circle, holding in their hands the staves of the loud-voiced heralds. Therewith then would they spring up and give judgement, each in turn. And in the midst lay two talents of gold, to be given to him whoso among them should utter the most righteous judgement.[15]

---

[15] Transl. A. T. M u r r a y, for the translation and the note with the commentary see: *The Iliad,* LOEB, Cambridge Mass.- London 1957, vol. II, pp. 324-325.

On the shield of Achilles, among many miraculous scenes, we see the picture of a city and its every-day life. The interpretation of the scene presented above has been discussed for a very long time. It may look quite simple, but a closer examination reveals several difficulties.[16] The simplest description of the situation goes as follows: many people have gathered in the agora to be present during the quarrel between two men whose argument is going to find the solution in front of a tribunal. One man tries to convince the judges that he did pay the fee for a killing, his opponent claims that he has never received any money. Both parties call witnesses, and they wait for the decision of the judges. The man who will prove to be the best judge and give the "straightest judgement" will be rewarded. The interpretation of V. Ehrenberg is close to this image.[17] According to his analysis, there are two men who bring their dispute in front of an arbiter (Schiedsrichter) in order to finish it. In the presence of the people, the elders (Geronten) sit in the holy circle and give their judgement in turn ("sagen wechselweise ihr Urteil"). The only problem is connected with the meaning of ἴστωρ and its reference to the γέροντες. V. Ehrenberg finds it unclear whether ἴστωρ is an individual, who is the president of the court, or whether it is a name given to the elders as a united body. The meaning of δίκη seems to be clear: it is a judgement of a single judge, δικάζειν denotes the process of giving such δίκαι. One of these judgements is "the straightest" and it ends the dispute. It is not easy to establish to what extent other judgements are straight, but it is evident that "being straight" ("Gerade") is not the integral part of the original meaning of δίκη.

A much more exhaustive analysis of the famous scene was given by H. Hommel.[18] Some of his conclusions are similar to the brief sketch drawn by V. Ehrenberg, but H. Hommel's survey provides a more complex examination of the details and contains the most basic questions referring to the subject. H. Hommel observes that the picture in the "Iliad" is far from be-

---

[16] Henri and Micheline van Effenterre, in their analysis of Homeric scene of arbitration, do not even provide the translation of the passage claiming that there are too many ambiguous places in the text and too many possibilities to prepare a clear and coherent translation. They point out all the words and expressions that have more that one sense. See: H. & M. v a n E f f e n t e r r e, *Arbitrages Homériques,* Symposion 1993, pp. 2-15.

[17] V. E h r e n b e r g, *op. cit.,* pp. 55-58.

[18] H. H o m m e l, *Die Gerichtsszene auf dem Schild des Achilleus; zur Pflege des Rechts in Homerischen Zeit,* Symbolae B. II, Hildesheim-Zürich-New York 1988, pp. 46-82, see also W y g a n o w s k i, *op.cit.,* pp. 329-220: in his opinion *istor* means "the one, who knows". W y g a n o w s k i presumes that δίκη means judgement, but, in much wider sense, justice, since it role consists in restoring justice; such an opinion goes a little too far, but he is right, when he underlines the meaning of the procedure for the life of *polis.*

ing distinct and lacks precision. The fact why it is so can be explained very easily if we assume that, at this particular moment, Homer is depicting the reality of his own time and the audience need no further description to be able to understand the story.[19]

According to Hommel, the first problem is connected with the subject of the quarrel. There are two possibilities: a) one litigant is claiming he has paid the whole sum, whereas the other refuses to admit[20], b) one is assuring he has paid all, πάντα, the other is denies having received anything. H. Hommel himself chooses the second interpretation.[21] The translation of ἀναίνετο is crucial for the controversy and the grammar seems to support the first option: ἀναίνομαι means "to deny" when connected with a participle, in the cases it means "to refuse".[22] On the other hand, the adjective

---

[19] According to Hommel this is about 700 B. C.; see: H. H o m m e l, op.cit, p. 48.

[20] This interpretation is believed to be represented by the lawyers.

[21] His translation of the text goes as follows: der eine beteuerte, er hat alles bezahlt, indem er dies dem Volk deutlich zu machen versuchte; der andere aber leugnete, irgend etwas erhalten zu haben.op. cit., p. 49. The same version is accepted by Polish translators: I. W i e n i e w s k i, (Iliada, Kraków 1984, p. 363) and K. J e ż e w s k a (Iliada, BN II Nr 17, Wrocław-Warszawa-Kraków-Gdańsk-Łódź 1986, p. 445). The opposite view is supported by A. T. M u r r a y; op.cit., pp. 324-325: the one avowed that he had paid all, declaring his cause to the people, but the other refused to accept aught. The problem consists not in the fact whether or not the payment was done, but in the question whether such a settlement should be allowed at all.

[22] M. W. E d w a r d s in his commentary (see: The Iliad, a commentary, ed. by G. S. Kirk, vol. V, Books 17-20, p. 215, Cambridge 1995) points out that ἀναίνομαι with infinitive in Homer normally means "refuse" (to do something), although there are two places in the "Odyssey", 9.116 and 14.149, where it can be translated as "refuse (to admit the idea)", "deny". Moreover, μηδέν is the only correct word in this context, whereas the meaning "denied that he had received anything" would be expressed by οὐδέν. The next problem is connected with the meaning of εὔχομαι. The translation: "the one was claiming to have paid everything" was argued by E. B e n v e n i s t e, Le Vocabulaire des institutions indo-européennes, Paris 1969, vol. II, pp. 233-243. according to his analysis the correct meaning of εὔχομαι is "promise". However, M. W. Edwards followed the opinion of A. E. Raubitschek that in the epigrams εὐχόμενος means "claiming", and εὐξάμενος "having promised". So, the form of imperfect, made from the same stem, expresses the same sense as the defendant's εὔχομαι "I am claiming". Edwards' conclusion is that the defendant is claiming to have paid everything, whereas the other man refused to accept anything. He supports this view with a comparative analysis of legal procedures in the ancient Near Eastern and Mycenaean societies presented by R. W e s t b r o o k, see: The Trial Scene in the Iliad, Harvard Studies in Classical Philology XCIV (1992), pp. 53-76.. According to Westbrook the kinsmen of a killed man had a right to choose either to take revenge or to accept a ransom. " In disputed cases, a court would decide: a) whether revenge or ransom was appropriate (...), and either b) the appropriate limit of revenge; or c) the appropriate amount of the ransom to be paid." In this scene, the defendant is claiming the right to pay ransom

πάντα suggests that the dispute had already been settled once and the compensation had been imposed.[23] The same view is presented by H. J. Wolff, who stresses the fact that the defendant speaks first. Further, he believes that the family of the killed man, using some self-help, threaded the man responsible for the death with violence. So, the agreed compensation was not handed over or rejected. Now, the killer is seeking help at the tribunal. Wolff concludes was that the issue was whether the money had been handed over or not, since the word ἀποδοῦναι was a technical term for paying a debt already incurred.[24] The present controversy regards the fact of the payment. The other interpretation may require a more complex discussion. A. T. Murray claims that the situation is as follows: the first question that should be answered is whether or not the killer "is allowed to settle with the kinsfolk of the man slain by payment of a blood-price".[25] When this matter is decided by an umpire, or a "daysman", ἴστωρ, the case is referred to "the elders", γέροντες. This theory assumes the procedure consisting of two stages and it is not easy to explain when exactly the helpers were active. It also omits the word πάντα. If this word is taken into consideration, the conclusion seems to be inevitable: the question whether or not the money can be a compensation for the killing had already been answered. Furthermore, to corroborate the interpretation of A. T. Murray one must know exactly what was the meaning and the role of the ἴστωρ. G. Thür assumes that the most probable issue of the dispute is whether the defendant had paid the compensation, although his translation of the passage seems to be inconsistent with this interpretation.[26] The word ἴστωρ causes some difficulties as well. The traditional and most popular translation is "one who knows", or "arbiter". The next question that arises here is the one concern-

full (πάντα), the amount to be fixed by the court, the other man is choosing the right to take revenge. The court is supposed to set the limit (πεῖραρ) of the penalty.

[23] A. Primmer, in his interesting article, concludes that the word πάντα is the only proof in favour of Hommel's interpretation. If the ποινή had been only an offer, it would have been called αἴσιμα πάντα or ἀπερείσια. According to his survey other arguments are false. See: A. P r i m m e r, *Homeriche Gerichtsszenen*, Wiener Studien 83 (1970), pp. 5-13.

[24] H. J. W o l f f, *The Origin of Judicial Litigation among the Greeks,* Traditio 4 (1946), pp. 31-87. The arguments presented by Wolff were also discussed by A. P r i m m e r, *op.cit.*, pp. 5-13.

[25] A. T. M u r r a y, *op. cit.,* p. 324, see above: M. W. Edwards and Westbrook's opinion.

[26] G. T h ü r, *op.cit.*, pp. 66-67: *the one entreated that he had paid everything, proclaiming to the community, but the other refused to take anything;* this translation is not quite correct; it suggests that both sentences were spoken by the defendant, who claimed that the other had not taken the money offered to him. Such a translation cannot be sustained, because there are two clauses here, introduced by two particles: ὁ μὲν - ὁ δέ - and the opposition of two different subjects.

ing the relation between this arbiter and the elders whose role, though not quite distinct, is far better described. Is he the presiding person or a member of the elders? G. Thür proposes that ἴστωρ is just the deity or deities by whom the litigants are going to swear.[27] For H. Hommel he is "one who knows", "der Kundige".[28] The controversy between singular ἴστωρ and plural γέροντες should not be the main problem, since the words ἐπὶ ἴστωρι may be also understood as a usual expression, the equivalent of German " das Gestetz bestimmt" that can be referred to more than one rule.[29]

Wolff's opinion that ἴστωρ is this elder who wins the prize of two talents was criticised by W. R. Connor. He seems to follow the view of W. Leaf, according to whom ἴστωρ could be the man to whom both parties turn for the settlement of their dispute. After recognising the difficulty, this arbiter calls the elders and hands the case over to the tribunal. The whole scene would resemble the famous passage from "Eumenides" by Aeschylos (Eum. 470-489).[30]

This short summary of interpretations regarding the preliminary details of the scene proves how difficult it is to give a coherent and complete analysis of the subject. In our opinion, the most reasonable is the assumption that the strife regards the compensation for a killing, the amount of which was previously determined. The money was not handed over to the family of the dead man, either because the family did not accept it for some reason (for example, because it was not enough; in that case they must have changed their mind since the moment when the compensation was set), so the killer could claim that what he wanted to pay was all (πάντα), or because the killer did not pay the blood-price at all. Then, the case was brought in front of the elders. The role of the "ἴστωρ" remains uncertain: he is certainly "one who knows", but the text is to short for us to decide whether he is an arbiter who turns the case to the elders, or whether he is one of them.

These details seem of secondary importance when compared to the question of the real significance of the procedure itself. Almost all scholars agree that what we have here is a legal (or some would say "proto-legal")

---

[27] G. T h ü r, op.cit., p. 69.

[28] H. H o m m e l, op.cit., p. 52; the etymology of this word supports this view: ἴστωρ (*Ϝιδ-τωρ) is derived from the same root as οἶδα (see: P. Chanteraine); for the brief survey see: M. W. E d w a r d s , op. cit., pp. 216-217, who concludes that the relation between the ἴστωρ and the elders remains unclear. For Wolff, he is the winner of two talents. For a more detailed analysis see: H.& M. van E f f e n t e r r e, Arbitrages Homériques, Symposion 1993, pp. 2-10.

[29] H. H o m m e l, op.cit., p. 53.

[30] W. R. C o n n o r, The Histor in History, in: Nomodeiktes,Greek Studies in Honour of Martin Ostwald, ed. by R. M. Rosen and J. Farrell, Michgan 1993, pp. 3-15.

procedure. The differences consist in defining what exactly this expression means. The abundant opinions could be reduced to two main views: the first one, let us call it traditional, has recently been supported by M. Gagarin[31], the second is represented by G. Thür and stands in opposition to the former interpretations.[32]

M. Gagarin's theory has already been mentioned; the scene from Achilles' shield is one of the main arguments supposed to prove its accuracy. The most important aspect of the first lines of the passage is the fact that both sides of the conflict bring their dispute in front of the court (in public) voluntarily. Thus the scene meets at least two of the criteria described by Gagarin as essential for a legal procedure: the proceedings are public and voluntary. This was also pointed out by H.J. Wolff, but Gagarin does not agree with Wolff's theory of self-help used by the kinsmen of the killed man. According to Gagarin, there is no proof that a community or any of its representatives possessed the power to protect a killer, if the family of the deceased wanted to persecute him on their own. The fact that the killer speaks first is not enough to convince us that he is the one seeking the protection of the judge and bringing the case to the court. It seems more plausible that both litigants came to the court voluntarily. The elders constitute a body of individual judges from among whose opinions one will be chosen as the straightest. The elders are not a collegial body, the settlement that will become the final decision will be given by one of the judges. The symbol of their power is a sceptre held by the judge who speaks. It is said it is the sceptre of the heralds.[33] The process of decision-making is not very clear: most probably the elders, on having heard both parties, perhaps influenced by the opinion of crowd (there are "helpers" of both litigants present at the court) give their judgements in turns without any discussion or argument about the case. This process is described by the verb δικάζειν. One of these judgements is chosen as the straightest. Δίκη denotes a judgement given by an individual judge. It may be inferred from the passage that all the judgements of the elders can be called δίκαι. The question of their being right or wrong plays no role in that context. One of these δίκαι is going to be ἰθυντάτη, the straightest. There are a few problems connected with this interpretation: the first one concerns the criteria of the choice and the other refers to the question who is going to chose the straightest judge-

---

[31] M.G a g a r i n, op.cit., p. 26 ff.

[32] G. T h ü r, op.cit., p. 66 ff.

[33] The significance of the sceptre is pointed out by all the scholars, e.g.: Ehrenberg, Raaflaub, Hirzel, Wyganowski, and it will be described together with the meaning of the royal power the symbol of which it is in the main part.

ment. The additional, and, in our opinion, less important issue, is the prize of two talents: by whom and exactly for what it is supposed to be paid. M. Gagarin claims that the straightest δίκη is the one that is the most acceptable for both litigants.[34] The judgement could be chosen by the litigants or by them together with the public. Probably the opinions of the elders might influence this decision. The prize of two talents is to be given by the litigants to the elder who turns out to be the arbiter in their dispute. This interpretation resembles the conclusion of H. Hommel. However, both theories seem to cause difficulties: first and the most striking is the problem of reaching the compromise in the manner described above. It is not that easy to settle the strife, and what sort of judgement would satisfy both parties at the same time? If the quarrel regards the question whether the money has been paid, what sort of compromise is possible? The other possibility, namely, that the strife refers to the problem of accepting the set amount of money or rejecting it, or rejecting the possibility of compensation instead of a revenge, gives almost no opportunity of reaching a satisfactory agreement. M. Gagarin, aware of such difficulties, tries to build a more sophisticated theory of the strife. The simple question whether the money has been paid or not, appears too easy to verify to be handed over to the court.[35] One of the possible explanations could be the disagreement between the relatives of the killed man. In our opinion however, such a hypothesis is too complicated and there is no chance to prove it.

The opposite view presented by G.Thür is not as popular as the previously mentioned theories. Thür follows Wolff's interpretation as regards the self-help action, but his analysis of the famous scene goes far beyond the traditionally accepted opinion.[36]

In his article, Thür answers three questions: 1) who wins the prize 2) what is the meaning of δικάζειν and 3) who is the ἵστωρ? For the first subject, Thür rejects the solution of H. Hommel, that two litigants choose the winner together, and follows the opinion[37] that the leaders of the assembly go on discussing till no more objections arise and one proposal is agreed upon. That may be true for the assemblies, but not necessarily for the court, and the question of the winner still remains open. If the final proposal is, in a way, a result of a discussion, who wins the prize?

The answer for the second question is much more interesting. The meaning of δικάζειν is "to formulate an oath". That is what the elders are doing:

---

[34] M. G a g a r i n, op.cit., pp. 30-31.

[35] M. G a g a r i n, op.cit., p. 32 ff.

[36] G. T h ü r, op.cit., p. 66 ff.

[37] Presented by Larsen, according to T h ü r, op.cit., p. 66.

they formulate different oaths, trying to adjust the text of the oath to the case. The problem is: which of the litigants should swear and what the oath should be like? The solution seems a little odd, but the procedure of taking oaths is proved in the history of Greek law. The settlement of the strife by swearing an oath would imply the divine factor: the power of an oath is due to the divine sanction standing behind it. For a religious man, a god's wrath, in the case of perjury was quite a real danger.

The third question has already been answered, the ἴστωρ is just the deity by whom the men are going to swear.

The whole theory seems to be coherent and plausible, nevertheless, there are some reasonable doubts regarding this interpretation. Partly they have been expressed by M. Gagarin. He formulates several statements referring to the earlier article by G. Thür[38], but the most important objection that can be applied to the theory discussed above is the fact that leaving the settlement of a strife between mortals entirely in the hands of the gods seems to be absent from Greek thinking in Homeric epic. Perhaps the oaths could play an auxiliary role in the proceeding, but it is hardly possible that they are the essence of it. The translation of ἴστωρ is also doubtful, since the presence of a mortal arbiter would come as no surprise. The question regards his position and details of his work, but the existence of such a "daysman" would be quite natural.

No matter, how interesting G. Thür's theory is, in our opinion the more traditional view, even full of obscure details, is more plausible.

The second passage, important for the analysis, comes from the book 23 (Il. 23. 566-585):

> Τοῖσι δὲ καὶ Μενέλαος ἀνίστατο θυμὸν ἀχεύων
> Ἀντιλόχῳ ἄμοτον κεχολωμένος· ἐν δή ἄρα κῆρυξ
> χειρὶ σκῆπτρον ἔθηκε, σιωπῆσαί τε κέλευσεν
> Ἀργείους· ὃ δή ἔπειτα μετηύδα ἰσόθεος φώς·
> Ἀντίλοχε πρόσθεν πεπνυμένε ποῖον ἔρεξας.
> ἤσχυνας μὲν ἐμὴν ἀρετήν, βλάψας δέ μοι ἵππους
> τοὺς σοὺς πρόσθε βαλών, οἵ τοι πολὺ χείρονες ἦσαν.
> ἀλλ᾽ ἄγετ᾽ Ἀργείων ἡγήτορες ἠδὲ μέδοντες
> ἐς μέσον ἀμφοτέροισι δικάσσατε, μὴ δ᾽ ἐπ᾽ ἀρωγῇ,
> μή ποτέ τις εἴπῃσιν Ἀχαιῶν χαλκοχιτώνων·
> Ἀντίλοχον ψεύδεσσι βιησάμενος Μενέλαος
> οἴχεται ἵππον ἄγων, ὅτι οἱ πολὺ χείρονες ἦσαν

---

[38] G. T h ü r, *Zum dikadzein bei Homer*, Zeitschrift der Savigny Stiftung, 87, pp. 426-444.

ἵπποι, αὐτὸς δὲ κρείσσων ἀρετῇ τε βίῃ τε.
εἰ δ᾽ ἄγ᾽ ἐγὼν αὐτὸς δικάσω, καί μ᾽ οὔ τινά φημι
ἄλλον ἐπιπλήξειν Δαναῶν· ἰθεῖα γὰρ ἔσται.
Ἀντίλοχή εἰ δ᾽ ἄγε δεῦρο διοτρεφές, ἦ θέμις ἐστί,
στὰς ἵππων προπάροιθε καὶ ἅρματος, αὐτὰρ ἱμάσθλην
χερσὶν ἔχε ῥαδινήν, ᾗ περ τὸ πρόσθεν ἔλαυνες,
ἵππων ἁψάμενος γαιήοχον ἐννοσίγαιον
ὄμνυθι μὴ μὲν ἑκὼν τὸ ἐμὸν δόλῳ ἅρμα πεδῆσαι.

Then among them uprose also Menelaus, sore vexed at heart, furiously wroth at Antilochus; and a herald gave him the staff into his hand, and proclaimed silence among the Argives; and thereafter spake among them the godlike man:

"Antilochus, thou that aforetime wast wise, what a thing hast thou wrought! Thou hast put my skill to shame and hast thwarted my horses, thrusting to the front thine own that were worser far. Come now, ye leaders and rulers of the Argives, judge ye aright betwixt us twain, neither have regard unto either, lest in aftertime some one of the brazen-coated Achaeans shall say": "Over Antilochus did Menelaus prevail by lies, and depart with the mare, for that his horses were worser far, but himself the mightier in the worth and in power". Nay, but I will myself declare the right, and I deem that none other of the Danaans shall reproach me, for my judgement shall be just. Antilochus, fostered by Zeus, up, come thou hither and, as it is appointed way, stand thou before thy horses and chariot, and take in hand the slender lash with which aforetime thou wast wont to drive, and laying thy hand on thy horses swear by him that holdeth and shaketh the earth that not of thine own will didst thou hinder my chariot by guile.[39]

The scene seems to be so important that it was crucial to quote it almost in full length. The description given by Homer does not make the analysis clear, although we are able to imagine the picture quite vividly. The multiplicity of the details does not explain the significance of the proceedings, which probably was obvious for the audience in the time of Homer.

The beginning of the scene is not unusual: Menelaus stands up in order to speak, so he is given a sceptre. In this moment, the sceptre in hand signifies the permission to speak in public.[40] Then the king asks for the assist-

---

[39] Transl. A. T. M u r r a y, *op.cit.*, vol. II, pp. 535-537.

[40] The symbolic role of a sceptre will be discussed later, in the next chapter. The significance of this instrument cannot be omitted while speaking about the role of a king. A sceptre is the visible symbol of royal might and authority. This is also the sign of the heralds; it denotes their function and, in a sense, gives them immunity. When someone

ance of the present Greek leaders in the case between him and Antilochus. It seems to be obvious that Menelaus believes the Greeks would be impartial. Up to this line the text appears to be free from confusion: Menelaus submits the case to the others, who are supposed to act as arbiters. His action is voluntary and he is probably going to accept the decision of the Greeks, although there is no proof that the arbiters had any power to induce their decision.[41] Menelaus is seeking a compromise and that is what eventually happens. The meaning of the word δικάσσατε is clear: to judge, or, to be more precise, to proclaim the judgement, "urteilen".[42] The behaviour of Menelaus is what could be expected in such a situation: it was always the litigant, the one who had been wronged by someone, who brought the case in front of the judges. K. Latte pointed out that the sense of this settlement of the dispute was not only to prove to the judges one's right, but to prove it to one another **in front of** the judges.[43] According to this scholar, the aim of the peaceful settlement of disputes, voluntary submission to the decision of the arbiters, or judges, was to prevent violence and self-help.[44] As a matter of fact, in this case the dispute is settled by the parties themselves, without any intervention of the arbiters.[45] Antilochus' speech is subtle and concentrates on the compliments towards Menelaus, to whom he gives the award not because the victory was unjust, but because, for a young knight the favour of a mighty king is far more valuable than the mare. In the end, Menelaus gives the horse back to Antilochus and the dispute finds its end peacefully.

What is really difficult and doubtful in this scene is the middle part of Menelaus' speech and the procedure proposed by him. The expression used by Menelaus, ἐγὼν αὐτὸς δικάσω, needs further explanation. According to

---

wishes to speak during the meeting, the herald gives him the sceptre transferring, for the time of the speech, a part of his own authority to the speaker.

[41] K. Latte stresses the fact that the judges have no force to make the litigants obey their decision. Their verdict is not compulsory in the present meaning of this word. It is accepted thanks to the willingness of both parties because of their mutual will to reach the compromise and their respect for the custom. See: K. L a t t e, *Der Rechtsgedanke im archaischen Griechentum,* Antike und Abendland, B. II (1946), pp. 63-76. On the other hand, the arbitration was not always successful: the best example is the rejection is the scene from the book 9th of the "Iliad" when Achilles turns down the proposal of reconciliation made by Agammemnon (Il. 9. 315-316).

[42] The same meaning is supported by K. L a t t e (*op.cit.*, p. 65), V. E h r e n b e r g, (*op. cit.,* pp. 56-57), M. G a g a r i n, (*op.cit.*, pp. 38-39).

[43] K. L a t t e, *op.cit.*, p. 67.

[44] *Ibidem.*

[45] M. G a g a r i n, *op.cit.*, p. 37 ff.

A. Primmer[46], the intention of Menelaus is to stress his conviction that he is right and that he has no doubt as to the decision of the judges. He is so sure of this that he could tell the judgement himself (αὐτὸς δικάζειν). This certainty does not mean that Menelaus does not recognize the authority of the judges. On the contrary, he need not fear that someone might criticise him; the case is clear. That is probably the reason why he decides to take the initiative and demand the oath from Antilochus. Some scholars claim that δικάζειν means just to propose the settlement and that by doing it Menelaus behaves as a king, to whom the authority to judge belonged.[47] It would mean that in this scene Menelaus plays a double role: this of a litigant and that of a judge. This opinion does not seem quite true. As a man who brings the case, Menelaus has the opportunity to make some proposals as to the settlement and doing so he does not change his position, but acts according to the custom. Quarrelling parties, or at least one of them, are able to take initiative and try to solve the problem themselves. That should be done in public, like in the case of Agamemnon and Achilles, and can be done in front of the judges who would probably take over the initiative if the attempts of the litigants were inefficient.

H. J. Wolff claims that the whole scene together with the passage where Antilochus protests against Achilles' decision to give the award for the second place to Eumelus (Il. 23. 539-554), can be explained as the use of self-help.[48] A. Primmer, commenting on these lines[49], suggests that Wolff's interpretation can be applied only to the passage referring to the protest of Nestor's son, because the young knight threatens the others with violence in case someone intends to take the horse away from him (Il. 23. 553-554):

τὴν δ' ἐγὼ οὐ δώσω; περὶ δ' αὐτῆς πειρηθήτω
ἀνδρῶν ὅς κ' ἐθέλῃσιν ἐμοὶ χείρεσσι μάχεσθαι.

The reaction of Menelaus while compared with these lines shows a few important differences: Menelaus brings his case in front of the arbiters, he does not say a single word of threat, his argument is based on the right, not on force and, as it has already been said, he does not reject the authority of the Greek leaders. According to the self-help theory, the verb δικάζειν used by Menelaus means that the king gives judgement in his own case. However, if it were the right interpretation, why does Menelaus ask the fellow-leaders for a judgement at all? This request is understandable only if one

---

[46] A. P r i m m e r, op.cit., p. 6 ff.
[47] E. W o l f, Griechiesches Rechtsdenken, Frankfurt am Main 1950, B. I, p. 88 ff.
[48] H. J. W o l f f, op.cit., p. 44 ff., p. 73 ff.
[49] A. P r i m m e r, op.cit., p. 5 ff.

presumes that Menelaus wants to hear the decision of the judges. However, he is so confident that the judgement would be in his favour that he could pronounce it himself.

The proposal of the oath reminds us of G. Thür's theory.[50] In his opinion, there is no doubt that the meaning of Menalaus' δικάζειν is "to formulate an oath", which is the correct way to settle the dispute. The authority of Poseidon as the master of horses and races who can easily punish the perjurer is comparable to the power that Artemis possessed towards women.

No one tries to deny the special might of the god and the significance of the oath, but it is not equivalent to the statement that oaths were the only way to settle contentions and that the role of the judges consist in nothing but formulating an oath. In particular case, this could be done by one of the parties. The oath proposed by the king of Sparta seems to be just the first attempt to solve the problem, but plays the role of an auxiliary factor. The oath is not the only way to finish the quarrel, as the scene describing Antilochus' protest proves. When Menelaus says that he will judge himself, αὐτὸς δικάσω, he means that he can produce the judgement in this case and, at all probability, the very same judgement as the one that would be given by the Greeks. The case is so distinct that what he does is merely anticipating the decision of the Greek leaders. Calling Antilochus to swear the oath is just a very simple way to prove that a king is right, but it is not the essential meaning of δικάζειν. The traditional opinion that Menelaus tends to use the normally accepted trial procedure seems to be the right one.[51]

The meaning of δίκη closely connected with this kind of procedure is that, which we can find in the book 19 (Il. 19. 172-183):

τὰ δὲ δῶρα ἄναξ ἀνδρῶν Ἀγαμέμνων
οἰσέτω ἐς μέσσην ἀγορήν, ἵνα πάντες Ἀχαιοὶ
ὀφθαλμοῖσιν ἴδωσι, σὺ δὲ φρεσὶ σῆσιν ἰανθῆς.
ὀμνυέτω δέ τοι ὅρκον ἐν Ἀργείοισιν ἀναστὰς
μή ποτε τῆς εὐνῆς ἐπιβήμεναι ἠδὲ μιγῆναι·
ἢ θέμις ἐστὶν ἄναξ ἤ τ' ἀνδρῶν ἤ τε γυναικῶν·
καὶ δὲ σοὶ αὐτῷ θυμὸς ἐνὶ φρεσὶν ἵλαος ἔστω.
αὐτὰρ ἔπειτά σε δαιτὶ ἐνὶ κλισίης ἀρεσάσθω
πιείρῃ, ἵνα μή τι δίκης ἐπιδευὲς ἔχῃσθα.

---

[50] G. T h ü r, op.cit., pp. 65-66.

[51] The same opinion is supported by A. Primmer and M. Gagarin who does not care to analyse the meaning of δικάζειν, but claims that the scenes from the book 23 illustrate the settlement of the dispute by compromise. (M. G a g a r i n, op.cit., p. 36 ff.).

'Ατρείδη σὺ δή ἔπειτα δικαιότερος καὶ ἐπ' ἄλλῳ
ἔσσεαι. οὐ μὲν γάρ τι νεμεσσητὸν βασιλῆα
ἄνδρ' ἀπαρέσσασθαι ὅτε τις πρότερος χαλεπήνῃ.

Odysseus comes to Achilles to ask him once more to forgive Agamemnon and let him honour Achilles with a feast. Achilles will not lose anything of δίκη. Gifts and behaviour of the king will make for the damage. Here δίκη signifies this what is right and just for Achilles, his due, this what he ought to receive. To fulfil the δίκη of Achilles, Agamemnon is not only going to give him precious gifts, including his daughter, seven cities and wealth, but he is also ready to swear the solemn oath that he did not touch Breseis. All this will be done in public, so that everyone can see it. The last element is extremely important: the reconciliation cannot be private, it must be witnessed by the people; this is what makes the proceeding valid. The gifts are necessary, because by taking Breseis away from the son of Peleus, Agamemnon injured the τιμή of Achilles. The respect for a knight was not only the matter of human memory and public opinion; it was shown quite practically by awarding a man with the gift of honour, i. e., with a part of the loot. The quantity of the gifts was the simplest measure of someone's position and his value. Breseis was the most prestigious part of such a gift. The loss of the girl was the loss of a part of τιμή.[52] To satisfy Achilles and his pride, Agamemnon would have to return the gift and add compensation. During the quarrel with the chief commander, Achilles lost something that he had earned and deserved, he had a right to such a gift and the respect connected with it. That was assigned to him according to the custom and public consent, so it was his δίκη.[53] The man who follows these demands and fulfils them can de described as δίκαιος, that is, one who gives to the others what is right.[54] In this sense Agamemnon on sending the gifts to Achilles has a chance to become δικαιότερος, more just as compared with his attitude in the beginning of the "Iliad".

This meaning of δίκη connected with the action taken by a king is supposed to belong to the older sphere.[55] In its significance we discover traces

---

[52] B. S n e l l, *Poetry and Society. The Role of Poetry in Ancient Greece,* Bloomington 1961, p. 14.

[53] This meaning is stressed by E. Wolf, who points out that δίκη is not only "what one deserves", but also the assigning and guarantee of this, see: E. W o l f, *op.cit.,* p. 85 ff. The same: V. E h r e n b e r g translates this term as "Anrecht", *op.cit.,* p. 55.

[54] E. W o l f, V. E h r e n b e r g, *ibidem.*

[55] Both V. Ehrenberg and E. Wolf describe some appearances of this term as being older, and some as belonging to the younger generation, but the explanation given by V. Ehrenberg is, in our opinion, more distinct, so we follow his interpretation.

of the time when the real power was the king and no one had a comparable authority. The term δίκη denoted the settlement of the dispute between a king a man. In this particular case the man is a king as well, but a minor one and subjected to the authority of Agamemnon.[56] The other passages where δίκη appears come from the period when the absolute power of a king was replaced by the aristocracy.

Nevertheless, there are passages where the meaning of δίκη resembles the sense mentioned above. The most adequate one comes from the book 23 (Il. 23. 546-547). After the race, which was a part of the celebrated contest to the memory of Patroclus, there is a controversy between the participants; Antilochus rises to claim his δίκη, this what, in his opinion, was due to him, what would be just.

εἰ μὴ ἄρ' Ἀντίλοχος μεγαθύμου Νέστορος υἱὸς
Πηλείδην Ἀχιλῆα δίκη ἠμείψατή ἀναστάς;

The new aspect of δίκη in that passage is connected with the situation itself: the goods promised to the winner of the second prize are given by one man, Achilles, and depend only on his decision. The reaction of Antilochus, when Achilles wants to give the award to someone else, is understandable. He uses the self-help to get what he believes is due to him. He is ready to fight with anyone who would try to take his award from him. This sort of reaction was not exceptional, and must have been acceptable: Achilles not only did not rebuke Nestor's son, but, as a matter of fact, the aggressive behaviour of Antilochus pleased the king of Myrmidons.

Δίκη in connection with the absolute royal authority, in the meaning of "decision of a king", appears only in one scene, Il. 16. 542, where Aeneas rebukes Hektor and recalls the brave Sarpedon, who Λυκίην εἴρυτο δίκῃσί τε καὶ σθένε ᾧ, protected Lycia with his decisions as well as his strength. The author of the commentary translates δίκαι as "just judgements".[57]

The other passages in the "Iliad" reflect the process of transition from the royal absolute authority to the rule of aristocracy.

---

[56] The source of royal authority, and, particularly, of Agamemnon, is Zeus himself. See: Il. 2. 196-197, 2. 204-206:
θυμὸς δὲ μέγας ἐστὶ διοτρεφέων βασιλήων,
τιμὴ δ' ἐκ Διός ἐστι, φιλεῖ δέ ἑ μητίετα Ζεύς.
οὐκ ἀγαθὸν πολυκοιρανίη; εἷς κοίρανος ἔστω,
εἷς βασιλεύς, ᾧ δῶκε Κρόνου πάϊς ἀγκυλομήτεω
σκῆπτρόν τ' ἠδὲ θέμιστας, ἵνά σφισι βουλεύῃσι.
[57] M. W. E d w a r d s, The Iliad, A Commentary, vol. 5, Cambridge 1991, p. 385.

Il. 1. 236-240

> περὶ γάρ ῥά ἑ χαλκὸς ἔλεψε
> φύλλά τε καὶ φλοιόν, νῦν αὖτέ μιν υἷες Ἀχαιῶν
> ἐν παλάμῃς φορέουσι δικασπόλοι, οἵ τε θέμιστας
> πρὸς Διὸς εἰρύαται

now the sons of the Achaeans that give judgement bear it (sceptre) in their hands, even they guard the dooms by ordinance of Zeus.[58]

The word δικασπόλος seems to be a technical term indicating the function of a judge, but the second line stresses the nature of that task; it appears to have a divine sanction. Zeus turns to be the source of a certain order; this fact makes us believe that the missions of δικασπόλος, law-maker, possessed some higher rank and cannot be treated as an ordinary office. Perhaps, the authority of the supreme god who used to support "kings nourished by Zeus" now protects the decision taken by the judges.

The moral aspect of the process of law-making becomes more evident in the well-known storm-simile in the book sixteen describing the intensifying Trojan rout, which reminds us of a rain-fed river in flood, destroying everything ahead of it:

Il.16. 384-393

> ὡς δ' ὑπὸ λαίλαπι πᾶσα κελαινὴ βέβριθε χθὼν
> ἤματ' ὀπωρινῷ, ὅτε λαβρότατον χέει ὕδωρ
> Ζεύς, ὅτε δή ῥ' ἄνδρεσσι κοτεσσάμενος χαλεπήνῃ,
> οἳ βίῃ εἰν ἀγορῇ σκολιὰς κρίνωσι θέμιστας,
> ἐκ δὲ δίκην ἐλάσωσι θεῶν ὄπιν οὐκ ἀλέγοντες·
> τῶν δέ τε πάντες μὲν ποταμοὶ πλήθουσι ῥέοντες,
> πολλὰς δὲ κλιτῦς τότ' ἀποτμήγουσι χαράδραι,
> ἐς δ' ἅλα πορφυρέην μεγάλα στενάχουσι ῥέουσαι
> ἐξ ὀρέων ἐπικάρ, μινύθει δέ τε ἔργ' ἀνθρώπων;

The power of Zeus punishing bad judges for crooked verdicts suggests a more optimistic image of the Homeric world than that to which we are accustomed. This bears a close resemblance to Hesiod, so in the eyes of many a scientist it became suspected.[59] For V. Ehrenberg it is the sign of a new period. It is close to Hesiod, but that does not have to be explained by interpolation. Nevertheless, the interpretation of these lines should be per-

---

[58] Trans. A. T. M u r r y, Homer, *The Iliad with English Translation by A.T. Murry,* LOEB, vol.1, 1954, (All the translations of the "Iliad" in this text come from this edition).

[59] A. D i c k i e, *Dike as a Moral Term in Homer and Hesiod,* CPh 73, pp. 91-101, R. J a n k o, The Iliad: A Commentary, *op.cit.,* pp. 335-336.

formed apart from the rest of the text.[60] V. Ehrenberg explains the ambiguous expression σκολιαὶ δίκαι explaines by the ethymology of the term δίκη. It was already mentioned that according to his theory, this word comes from the root δικ-, δικεῖν, "to throw". The basic meaning of δίκη would be "a throw" and that explains the adjectives σκολιός, ἰθύς. Although this theory seems to be logical, most sources do not support it. We also find the opposite view, namely that the term's root is δεικ-, more persuasive. Scholars who do not believe that in Homer we do deal with some moral ideas, try to prove that it is a later interpolation. According to the anthropological theory of E.R. Dodds[61], neither in the "Iliad" nor in the "Odyssey" δίκη, or any other term, deserves the name of a true moral concept, since the Greek society of that time belongs to the so called shame-culture. People choose certain forms of behaviour not guided by the inner sense of justice or by any consciously created hierarchy of values, but because they want to win the acceptance of other people. The fear of shame substitutes morality.

In this case, the first question that crosses one's mind is the basic question of any criterion upon which such public disapproval or acceptance could be supported. The presence of this kind of criterion is necessary, and it is obvious that it would make Dodd's theory questionable. To criticise other people's behaviour, one must have some knowledge of what is right and what is wrong.

In the analysis based on ethymology, also M.Gagarin tried to prove that δίκη and its derives in Homer are devoid of moral significance. According to his analysis, in the "Iliad" and the "Odyssey" δίκη means "characteristic", "characteristic behaviour" (this, in my opinion, is correct in a few places in the "Odyssey"), settlement" and "decision".[62] This conclusion seems to me partly true, but in some passages, like the one quoted above, moral significance of δίκη can be inferred from the text.

The use of the highest grade of the adjective δίκαιος brings other problems. In the "Iliad", there are only two lines where δίκαιος appears:
Il.11, 828- 832

> ἀλλ' ἐμὲ μὲν σὺ σάωσον ἄγων ἐπὶ νῆα μέλαιναν,
> μηροῦ δ' ἔκταμ' ὀϊστόν, ἀπ' αὐτοῦ δ' αἷμα κελαινὸν
> νίζ' ὕδατι λιαρῷ, ἐπὶ δ' ἤπια φάρμακα πάσσε
> ἐσθλά, τά σε προτί φασιν Ἀχιλλῆος δεδιδάχθαι,
> ὃν Χείρων ἐδίδαξε δικαιότατος Κενταύρων.

[60] V. E h r e n b e r g, op.cit., p. 56 ff.
[61] E. R. D o d d s, The Greeks and the Irrational, Beacon Press, Boston 1957, pp. 1-28.
[62] M. G a g a r i n, op.cit., p. 36 ff.

and
Il.13. 1- 7

Ζεὺς (...)
αὐτὸς δὲ πάλιν τρέπεν ὄσσε φαεινὼ
νόσφιν ἐφ᾽ ἱπποπόλων Θρηκῶν καθορώμενος αἶαν
Μυσῶν τ᾽ ἀγχεμάχων καὶ ἀγαυῶν ἱππημολγῶν
Γλακτοφάγων ᾽Αβίων τε δικαιοτάτων ἀνθρώπων.
ἐς Τροίην δ᾽ οὐ πάμπαν ἔτι τρέπεν ὄσσε φαεινὼ

Cheiron, the Centaur, is perhaps called δικαιότατος in contrast with other Centaurs[63]. Nevertheless, it appears to bear at least an element of moral evaluation. We may learn from the text that Cheiron was Achilles' tutor, who taught him how to heal wounds[64].

The second passage, from the book 13, includes a mention about people called A-bioi, the name meaning "without violence".[65] It is easy to associate the idea of being just with refraining from violent acts, but still, in my opinion, we cannot identify one with another. The scene when Zeus, tired with the battle at Troy, gazes at δικαιότατοι ῎Αβιοι is worth remembering; perhaps we have got here the prophecy for the future. It is also possible that these few lines of the text could explain why in the "Iliad" no eminent hero was called δίκαιος. This virtue is not what counted in the time of a cruel war. It is too closely connected with maintaining proper relationships with other members of the same community and with people belonging to the same culture. This aspect of δίκαιος will be illustrated later, in the "Odyssey".

The most striking fact is that it is not easy to connect the use of the adjective δίκαιος in these two passages with any meaning of δίκη explained above. The only possibility is that both terms refer to the refraining from violence. It should be added that in the case of δίκη this is only one aspect of its sense. Furthermore, this term in the "Iliad" has mainly the concrete meaning, even the slight moral evaluation present in the storm-simile does not change this basic statement. On the other hand, all the instances of demanding or producing δίκη illustrate the proceedings aiming at a peaceful solution of a dispute[66].

---

[63] Kirk, op.cit.

[64] For the importance of this passage for the general image of Greek paideia, see: E. W o l f, op.cit., p. 92 ff.

[65] or "nomads" see Kirk, see also V. E h r e n b e r g, op.cit., p. 55.

[66] E. W o l f, op.cit., p. 91 ff: who has δίκη need not any violence. Wolf underlines also the similarity between Cheiron and Abioi: they do not belong to the Greek nation: the first

The lines quoted above were supposed to prove that the term δίκη in the "Iliad" has some moral qualifications. On the other hand, it is easy to omit it if one takes into consideration other places where δίκη appears.

The last, and perhaps the less complicated use of δίκη in the "Iliad" refers to the process of decision-making, and does not necessarily regard judgement as a legal process (Il. 1. 540-543):

τίς δ' αὖ τοι δολομῆτα θεῶν συμφράσσατο βουλάς
αἰεί τοι φίλον ἐστὶν ἐμεῦ ἀπὸ νόσφιν ἐόντα
κρυπτάδια φρονέοντα δικαζέμεν οὐδέ τί πώ μοι
πρόφρων τέτληκας εἰπεῖν ἔπος ὅττι νοήσῃς.

When Hera rebukes her husband for hiding some decisions from her, she most probably does not mean any decision of a particularly legal character. We may also assume that these decisions are not necessarily based on any moral criterion. Zeus is going to decide who will win and who will loose. This, however, depends generally on his attitude towards people whose lives he keeps in his hands. To some scholars, the activity of Zeus resembles the occupation of an arbiter who assigns the lot to each party of the dispute.[67] Such an opinion would support the general statement according to which the meaning of δίκη in the first Homeric epic is usually connected with the principle of judgement. This however, can be also applied to the process of deciding in various cases not necessarily referring to the legal action.

The analysis presented above is supposed to lead to the very general conclusion: the notion δίκη as well as its derivatives are used in the relatively broad sense. No single and simple definition could be ascribe to these terms. The most basic intuition points at the sphere of the mutual relations connecting men living in a community. This is the first step in the process at the end of which δίκη became one of the most important moral notions in the Greek thought. At the time of Homer its meaning was in a great part limited to the concrete sense defined in the particular circumstances, nevertheless, some passages show the beginning of the abstract thinking.

---

one is a creature being partly a human and partly an animal, the latter are barbarians. So, their being δίκαιοι has nothing to do with judgements or right, it has nothing in common with the Greek way of life depicted in the "Iliad". We cannot verify Wolf's statement that Abioi, like Cyclops, do not know meetings, rights and other elements of Hellenic culture, but they probably are different and do not live in a way practised by Homeric Greeks.

[67] For instance: V. E h r e n b e r g, op.cit., p. 57.

Δίκη in the "Odyssey".

The moral concepts in the later Homeric epic opens the way for various interpretations. The image of the world described in the "Odyssey" takes us to the period of great changes and transformation. It is a generally accepted view that the "Odyssey" was composed in the epoch of colonization.[1] The human being portrayed in the poem corresponds to the conditions of the time. A hero did not lose his courage or his great heart, but he used them as complementary to his intellect, wits and common sense.[2]

The main conflict, around which the whole story is composed, differs from that known from the "Iliad".[3] Instead of two noble men, whose ambitions pushed them against each other and whose quarrel finally found a peaceful solution, in the "Odyssey" the hero stands opposite the men of a much lower quality. Their behaviour leads them straight to the doom. Their character and will are tested several times, unfortunately they do not realise the danger connected with wrong deeds and they lose all the opportunities of salvation. The poem describing the history of a good man fighting the hardships of his fate and his victory over unjust enemies must represent a much higher level of moral wisdom than the story of a fierce battle. The concept of morality and justice of the "Odyssey" may be concentrated around one rule, which seems to be a source of almost all other laws. The role of such dominance in the "Odyssey" is played by the law of hospitality. We

---

[1] There are surveys proving that the "Odyssey" contains not only motifs taken from the myths of the Greek world and the epic reflects different folktale motifs; the best example is the story of Poliphemus, see: D. P a g e, *The Homeric Odyssey,* Oxford 1955. This fact makes us believe that the knowledge of the world and people living in different lands was spread out. The heroes depicted by Homer, as well as the audience, belonged to the world which comprised diverse lands, people and ways of life. The Greeks, consciously or not, were apart of these universe and built their cultural identity in accordance with other elements, or in opposition to them.

[2] The research conducted by D. Frame proved strong relations binding the symbol of return, νόστος, with the activity of mind, νόος. The basic meaning of the return is "returning to life and light". In the epic, there are episodes in which it is clear that the real way of return from the death to the life leads through the power of mind, i. e., Circe. For a detailed analysis see: D. F r a m e, *The Myth of Return in Early Greek Epic,* Yale-New Heven-London 1978, pp. 34-53.

[3] H a v e l o c k, *The Greek Concept of Justice,* Cambridge, Mass. 1978, pp. 9-15.

are prone to say that an analysis of the term δίκη must refer to that point as well. It also seems justified to ask about the reason why this law occupies the highest position. In our opinion, the answer is strictly connected with the reality of that world. The Mediterranean is inhabited by Greeks and people similar to the Greek. They live in cities and they travel a lot. At least a part of the community is mobile for numerous purposes; they travel to see new people, make noble friends and learn something new; they make business and earn money; sometimes they are made to leave their mother land because of something they have done. Considering the case of Telemachus, we may have an impression that a journey is a sort of exam for a young man. What may be a little surprising is the fact that in spite of all the relations binding people from different cities, including friendship between the rulers, there is no official relation between cities.[4] In such a situation people leaving their country can count only on themselves or on the friendly hosts. In the ancient world, where a journey might easily turn to be a disaster, hospitality was the condition of co-existence. It was the only way to assure safety far from home. Such an attitude made it possible to travel and, what follows, to exchange information and knowledge. This became the fundamental factor of progress. Being such an important rule, the law of hospitality was guarded by the most important and powerful god. Harming a guest meant violating the τιμή of Zeus Xenios. Another aspect of that rule was the law protecting an impoverished man, a beggar. In order to test the loyalty and the character of his family, household and the suitors, Odysseus comes home as a miserable beggar, asking for help and protection.

The term δίκη appears in the formula repeated several times by the hero at the moment when, on reaching an unknown land, Odysseus feels uncertain of what the future may bring. When he is thrown on the seashore of

---

[4] M. I. Finley underlines the importance of counter-gifts exchanged between men from different cities as the symbol of the law of hospitality. Protection of a powerful friend, a king, gave the support and assistance, even military help. The basis for such relations which, in modern terminology, belong to foreign affairs was personal bounds created by mutual respect for the law of hospitality. The informal rules that governed the delicate matters of hospitality were complicated, because there was a special order and code of conduct, for instance: one had to know to whom he can offer his gifts and from whom he can accept them. All that was based on hierarchy and tact. The relationship of hospitality was treated very seriously and the institution of a guest-friend played an extremely important role in the society, where the natural feeling of hostility and distrust dominated in the relations between men coming from different cities. See: M. I. F i n l e y, *The World of Odysseus*, London 1956, pp. 106-112. V. Ehrenberg also underlines the proper treatment of strangers as the most important aspect of being δίκαιος. The very direct association is just "to treat

Scheria[5], helpless and looking for a shelter, Odysseus asks himself in despair (Od. 6. 119-121):

> ὤ μοι ἐγώ, τέων αὖτε βροτῶν ἐς γαῖαν ἱκάνω
> ἦ ῥ' οἵ γ' ὑβρισταί τε καὶ ἄγριοι οὐδὲ δίκαιοι,
> ἦε φιλόξεινοι καί σφιν νόος ἐστὶ θεουδής

Alas, to the land of what mortals have I now come? Are they cruel, and wild and unjust? or are they kind to strangers and fear the gods in their thoughts?[6]

It is easy to notice that there is no exact form of the negative adjective "unjust"; in the text there is a negation and "δίκαιοι". Being δίκαιος seems to depend in to a large extent on the attitude towards strangers and gods. As we have already mentioned, these two elements were not perceived separately. This question is the very first thought that crosses one's mind in a foreign country. The man proves that he is δίκαιος by proper treatment of a stranger-guest, like the son of Nestor, Peisistratus, who gains the esteem of Athene in that way (Od. 3. 52-54):

> χαῖρε δ' 'Αθηναίη πεπνυμένῳ ἀνδρὶ δικαίῳ,
> οὕνεκα οἱ προτέρη δῶκε χρύσειον ἄλεισον;
> αὐτίκα δ' εὔχετο πολλὰ Ποσειδάωνι ἄνακτι;

and Pallas Athene rejoiced at the man's wisdom and decorum, in that to her first he gave the golden cup; and at once she prayed earnestly to the lord Poseidon.

The reason why the goddess, who accompanied Telemachus as Mentor, appreciated the behaviour of Peisistratus, was the fact that the prince of Pylos first gave a cup of wine to her, the older of two strangers. Obviously, we may assume that Athene knew Nestor's son and his virtue, but in this line δίκαιος refers mainly to the proper treatment of a guest. The gesture of Peisistratus cannot be understood only as a mere courtesy of a well educated man. In the translation of A.T. Murray we find two words: wisdom and decorum. Peisistratus is the son of Nestor, an old king whose reason-

---

strangers without violence and to protect them". The opposite is called: ἄγριοι, ὑβρισταί. see: V. E h r e n b e r g, *Die Rechtsidee im frühen Griechentum,* Leipzig 1921., p. 60 ff.

[5] The island of Phaeacians is a special place; it is often underlined that Scheria had features of Utopia; one of the most important details is the complete isolation of this land. M. I. F i n l a y, *op.cit.,* pp. 110.

[6] Transl. A.T. Murray, see: Homer, *The Odyssey,* with an English translation, LOEB Classical Library, London 1995.

able advice and noble life became widely known. Now, the young generation of this family proves his quality. The praise for the kindness comes immediately, although neither the noble king nor his children realise it. Athene herself prays to the lord Poseidon for the good future for her host and his family. The conclusion is clear: be δίκαιος and you will find the grace of the god.

This belief is shared and expressed also by other characters of the poem. Eumaeus, the kind-hearted and loyal swineherd, after having accepted a stranger-beggar into his shed invites him to dinner with the words (Od.14. 80-86):

> ἔσθιε νῦν, ὦ ξεῖνε, τά τε δμώεσσι πάρεστι,
> χοίρε᾽; ἀτὰρ σιάλους γε σύας μνηστῆρες ἔδουσιν,
> οὐκ ὄπιδα φρονέοντες ἐνὶ φρεσὶν οὐδ᾽ ἐλεητύν.
> οὐ μὲν σχέτλια ἔργα θεοὶ μάκαρες φιλέουσιν,
> ἀλλὰ δίκην τίουσι καὶ αἴσιμα ἔργ᾽ ἀνθρώπων.

He is a little bit ashamed about what he is able to offer to his guest, and we have already found out how important it is for him to honour a stranger (Od. 14. 46-59):

> πρὸς γὰρ Διός εἰσιν ἅπαντες ξεῖνοί τε πτωχοί τε.

He would like to give something more to his guest. In spite of his position (Eumaeus is a slave) and his bitter lot, he strongly believes in the divine judgement. Σχέτλια ἔργα of the suitors will not please the gods who love δίκη.

In this context δίκη expresses more than hospitality. Yet, appropriate treatment of a stranger and fear of gods' wishes constitute a greater part of it.

Eumaeus' opinion draws our attention to the negative example of people who respect neither divine orders nor human rules. The abominable behaviour of Penelope's suitors is going to cause their miserable end. They have been given a chance to avoid the final disaster, but they do not want to use it. They are called fools. In the second book of the "Odyssey" we meet this opinion for the first time (Od. 2. 283-286):

> τῷ νῦν μνηστήρων μὲν ἔα βουλήν τε νόον τε
> ἀφραδέων, ἐπεὶ οὔ τι νοήμονες οὐδὲ δίκαιοι;
> οὐδέ τι ἴσασιν θάνατον καὶ κῆρα μέλαιναν,
> ὡς δή σφιν σχεδόν ἐστιν ἐπ᾽ ἤματι πάντας ὀλέσθαι.

Now therefore put from your mind the suitors' plans and intentions - fools, for they are in no way either prudent or just. Nor are they at all

*aware of the death and black fate, which in truth is near at hand for them;
to die all one day.*[7]

The suitors are *οὔ τι νοήμονες οὐδὲ δίκαιοι*; in no way prudent or just. They
did not agree to Telemachus' proposal presented in the meeting.

The very same epithet referred to the Achaean soldiers who were punished by the gods when they left Troy (Od. 3. 130-134):

αὐτὰρ ἐπεὶ Πριάμοιο πόλιν διεπέρσαμεν αἰπήν,
[βῆμεν δ' ἐν νήεσσι, θεὸς δ' ἐκέδασσεν 'Αχαιούς,]
καὶ τότε δὴ Ζεὺς λυγρὸν ἐνὶ φρεσὶ μήδετο νόστον
'Αργείοισή, ἐπεὶ οὔ τι νοήμονες οὐδὲ δίκαιοι
πάντες ἔσαν;

We may get an impression that there the meaning of δίκαιος was slightly
changed; some new aspects appeared in that word. Δίκαιος means: "he who
knows where lies the boundary dividing that, what can be done by a mere
mortal, and what is forbidden for him".

The meaning of the δίκαιος was slightly changed since the time of the
"Iliad", where it described a man who knew and fulfilled δίκη. The concrete significance and the more or less straight-forward relation to the noun
was loosened, and δίκαιος became a term connected with the norms of aristocratic society.[8] The extremely important aspect of this term is the divine
sanction as a guarantee for just men. The wrong-doers will be punished.
The text confirms this belief. There is a relation between death of the wooers
and their conduct; the missing element, absent in the "Iliad", finally appeared.

Among the derivatives of the word δίκη there are verbs, adjectives and
adverbs. The latter appear very seldom. In the book 14 (Od.14. 90-92), the
suitors οὐκ ἐθέλουσι δικαίως μνᾶσθαι οὐδὲ νέεσθαι ἐπὶ σφέτερ', ἀλλὰ ἔκηλοι
κτήματα δαρδάπτουσσιν ὑπέρβιον, οὐδ' ἐπὶ φειδώ.

The adverb δικαίως means: "fairly, properly".

In the book 20 there is an example of an adverbial use of the adjective
(Od. 20. 293-294):

οὐ γὰρ καλὸν ἀτέμβειν οὐδὲ δίκαιον
ξείνους Τηλεμάχου,

for it is not well or just to rob of their due the guests of Telemachus

---

[7] Transl. A.T. M u r r a y, *op.cit.*
[8] V. E h r e n b e r g, *op.cit.*, pp. 55 ff.

The formula is repeated twice. What we have got here is a straight-forward evaluation of an action; this does not appear in the epics too often. In the second passage this is also connected with the appropriate attitude towards a stranger entering one's house.

The wrong doings of the suitors consist mainly in damaging the honour of Telemachus and his father and in devouring his property. We may also consider their impudent behaviour in terms of the law of hospitality. They stay at the house of Odysseus as guests and they are obliged to respect the accepted code of behaviour, for the law of hospitality should be respected not only by the host but by the guest as well. The proper relationship between the guest and the host should be based on mutual trust. The older poem described the war that was caused by a violation of that rule. Paris's unlawful behaviour was considered quite a good reason to begin a war.

Another story of a broken law of hospitality is connected with Agamemnon and his wife. The part of the violator in this drama is performed by Aegisthus.

The young noblemen of Ithaka had the right to propose to Penelope, who, in their opinion, had already become a widow. However, they were not entitled to ruin the property of her son.

Still another, even more dreadful example of a bad conduct is the behaviour of Polyfphemus, the Cyclops, who belongs to a tribe knowing οὔτε δίκας οὔτε θέμιστας. He appears to be a savage beast, a monster, the most striking example of a barbarian creature. He and his fellow countrymen are described as uncivilized men who know nothing of laws or rights; this, of course, cannot be an excuse for their abominable crimes. It may be argued that the Cyclopes are a personification of the danger connected with the Unknown.[9] Every sailor, merchant or any other traveller must have been afraid of what or whom he might meet some day. On the other hand, the knowledge of δίκη and θέμιστες expresses the most important element of Greek identity.[10] This seems to be a proof of being a part of Hellenic, i.e.,

---

[9] The story about Cyclops belongs to the widely known motifs in the folktales. Similar tales existed in the tradition of diverse nations and in different periods. The main subject was to glorify a cunning man who when exposed to the ultimate danger, finds the way of salvation. See: D. P a g e, *op.cit.*, pp. 3-5.

Furthermore, there is the motif of a collision between the civilized and the uncivilized, mind and brutal force. Finally, the story may be interpreted as the symbol of returning from death to life. D. Frame found some features in the story, as well as in the tale of Laestrygonians, proving that the cave of Poliphemus was the world of the death. See: D. F r a m e, *op.cit.*, pp. 53-80.

[10] I cannot fully agree with W y g a n o w s k i, when he claims that the main difference between the Cyclopes and the Greek society consists in the absence of social procedure:

civilized world. Savage creatures like the Cyclopes or Laestrygons do not belong to that circle.

For M. I. Finley, the element of social evaluation plays an important role in the whole story; Cyclopes still live in the world of total hostility towards outsiders, they are a primitive tribe who did not discover the advantages of mutual bonds offered by the law of hospitality.[11] They live in isolation and are pleased with it. Their knowledge of the world is null and they are aware only at a very small degree of the differences between them and the world outside.

In the "Odyssey", the word δίκη and its derivatives usually associated with ξενία were also used to express the terms of judgement, like it was in the "Iliad".

Nestor, for instance, among other qualities and virtues is thought to be a good and just ruler, who "knows judgements and wisdom" (Od. 3. 244-246):

Νέστορ', ἐπεὶ περίοιδε δίκας ἠδὲ φρόνιν ἄλλων;
τρὶς γὰρ δή μίν φασιν ἀνάξασθαι γένε' ἀνδρῶν,
ὥς τέ μοι ἀθάνατος ἰνδάλλεται εἰσοράασθαι.

since beyond all others he knows judgements and wisdom; for three times, men say, has he been king for a generation of man, and like an immortal he seems to me to look upon

The old ruler, who had been reigning for three generations, acquired a great deal of practice and proved it many times trying to reconcile quarrelling men.[12] Δίκη as a peaceful solution of a controversy was a fundamental element and a condition without which the existence of a city would turn out impossible. The moment when people agreed to receive financial compensation for a damage instead of beginning a vendetta must have been the most important step towards a political community, a society of citizens. In the early ages of the ancient history, as the written law was not at hand yet, the ruler's personal ability and talent was crucial for preserving social order. Now it becomes perfectly understandable, why Nestor deserves so much attention. He is the ideal βασιλεύς; wise, prudent and just. These virtues are

---

θέμιστες and δίκαι bring order in the relations between particular families and this is the element the Cyclopes miss, while they can solve an argument inside one's own family. I do believe that the significance of the terms mentioned above is wider and their absence excludes any sot of civilized life.

[11] M. I. F i n l a y, *op.cit.*, pp. 111-112.

[12] See also: P. W y g a n o w s k i, *"Dike" u Homera,* Meander 7-8 (1994), pp. 327-340, p. 339.

the best guarantee of prosperity for his subjects. Nestor's knowledge comprises the rights of other people and the ways how to give them what is their due. Telemachus says to the king of Pylos: σὺ δ' ἀληθὲς ἐνίσπες, you pronounce the truth.[13]

In the text we also find a picture describing a judgement that takes place in Hades. This provokes some false connotations with Christian religion. (Od.11. 568-571):

> ἔνθ' ἦ τοι Μίνωα ἴδον, Διὸς ἀγλαὸν υἱόν,
> χρύσεον σκῆπτρον ἔχοντα θεμιστεύοντα νέκυσσιν,
> ἥμενον; οἱ δέ μιν ἀμφὶ δίκας εἴροντο ἄνακτα,
> ἥμενοι ἑσταότες τε, κατ' εὐρυπυλὲς Ἄϊδος δῶ.

I saw Minos, the glorious son of Zeus, golden sceptre in hand, giving judgement to the dead from his seat, while they sat and stood about the king in the wide-gated house of Hades and asked him for judgement.

Δίκη means here: decision, i.e., a verdict. The picture may be a little mystical, nevertheless the term δίκη is used as a technical term denoting the verdict in a legal procedure. Minos is performing exactly the same function as he used to perform while alive[14]: acting as a judge and, perhaps, as an arbiter between litigants. The picture is not too clear and probably the meaning of δίκη adheres to the older sphere, where it regarded the royal power. It is the king, not the aristocrats or the elders, who decides.

Finally, we arrive at the last point of this short survey. There is one more meaning of δίκη; for some scholars it is the most typical for Homer and the "Odyssey". Sometimes it is also included in one of the groups listed above: δίκη as a characteristic, custom, an appointed way, or, in a broader sense, "what is proper, what might be expected".[15] This usually refers to a group, not to an individual.

---

[13] V. E h r e n b e r g (*op.cit.*, pp. 58-59) underlines that aspect of his rule. Besides, he points at the words of Telemachos who says to the king of Pylos: σὺ δ' ἀληθὲς ἐνίσπες, you pronounce the truth. (Od. 3. 247). For Ehrenberg, this means that a king knows the truth, because the role of a judge and arbiter consists in finding the truth. Certainly, we may assume that the knowledge and wisdom of Nestor reveals to him the true nature of things, but we cannot consider the words of Telemachos out of the context. In the text, they are a part of his request for any information of Odysseus and do not refer directly to the royal might of Nestor. What the prince of Ithaka refers to, is Nestor's knowledge about the Trojan war and the lots of the Achaean knights.

[14] The same opinion was presented by W y g a n o w s k i, *op.cit.*, p. 337.

[15] V. Ehrenberg claims that the meaning of this expression is even broader: in part, it almost denotes the law of nature, something necessary (Od. 11.218, 19.43, 19. 168), in other passages it is closer to the expression of one's part, right (Od. 14.59, 18.275). "A

Od. 4. 689-691

οἷος Ὀδυσσεὺς ἔσκε μεθ᾽ ὑμετέροισι τοκεῦσιν,
οὔτε τινὰ ῥέξας ἐξαίσιον οὔτε τι εἰπὼν
ἐν δήμῳ ἤ τ᾽ ἐστὶ δίκη θείων βασιλήων;

what manner of man Odysseus was among them that begot you, in that he did no wrong in deed or word to any man in the land as the custom is of divine kings

Other popular expressions includes: δίκη ἐστί θεῶν, δίκη ἐστί γερόντων. The meaning of δίκη is the same as in the passage quoted above.

In that meaning the word δίκη does not necessarily denote any moral qualification. The best proof of it is the first fragment, where Penelope recalls the kindness of her husband who had never harmed anyone, although other kings did.

This is, however, not the most important way of using the word δίκη. We may presume that the examples listed above reflect a more significant role of this term. We are convinced that in a great part of the poem the meaning of δίκη and the words of the same family cannot be restricted to the so called technical, legal term. It may be inferred from the text that in the background the deeper sense of justice exists.

It seems to be connected with what was crucial to the contemporary man, what was decisive in the process of social relationships and what could be most important in a man's life.

We might underestimate the meaning of this term in Homer, because our own idea of justice is much more complex and comprises the tradition of 2000 years of western philosophy and Christian ethics. Perhaps for a modern man this simple definition, or rather description, of such an important notion seems too easy. Nevertheless we cannot ignore it, since for generations of our predecessors it used to stand for a moral criterion.

---

custom" is not the genuine meaning of this term, its significance developed from the term denoting "right to something". V. E h r e n b e r g, *op.cit.*, pp. 59-61.

Θέμις in the Homeric Iliad

The word θέμις[1] as well as the name of the goddess first appeared in Homeric epics. However, its too large a number of complex meanings suggests that its history is relatively long, as was already marked by Victor Ehremberg in his brilliant analysis of this notion.[2] In the "Iliad" we deal at least with five slightly different meanings of θέμις and there is also a goddess bearing the same name. As it is usually stated, we might solve the problem connected with Θέμις by assuming that the deity personifies the abstract sense of the word. Unfortunately, to such a solution we must pose at least two important objections. First, it would be difficult to prove that Homeric θέμις has already achieved this state of abstraction which makes it possible to draw a straight - forward connection to the name of a super-human power. Secondly: the word itself does not have a single, clear meaning; instead, it serves to show several senses in several definite situations.

The subject has long been discussed and we may conclude that there are three main opinions:

Rudolf Hirzel[3] quotes the statement of Grote's *History of Greece* (London 1946, II, 111), according to which the name of a god can be seen by metonyme in the word θέμις. R.Hirzel himself does not concede to it, although he stresses that the name of Themis is very helpful to the right understanding of the meaning of θέμις. As a matter of fact his analysis of various aspects of θέμις almost always has something to do with the way, in which he understands the role of the goddess.[4] Besides, his deeply interesting and profound interpretation of the divine nature of Themis is based not only on Homeric epics, but, it also uses more literary sources to produce a complete image of the deity.[5]

---

[1] Etymology of the word θέμις seems to be quite clear, but it used to be discussed by R. H i r z e l, (*Themis, Dike, und Verwandtes*, Hildesheim 1966), who had some doubts as to its traditional version. According to the *Griechisches Ethymologisches Worterbuch* by H. F r i s k (ed.Heidelberg 1954) θέμις comes from the stem da-mi - Schöpfer, da-ta - Satzung. The problems arises in plural form: θέμιστες.

[2] V. E h r e n b e r g, *Die Rechtsidee im fruhren Griechentum*, Leipzig 1921.

[3] R. H i r z e l, *Themis, Dike, und Verwandtes*, Hildesheim 1966.

[4] *Ibidem*, pp. 1-52.

[5] *Ibidem*, pp. 2-4.

V. Ehrenberg mentions the opinion[6] according to which both the term and the name of the goddess emerged at the same time, but he has hardly any doubts that such a situation might be possible. V.Ehrenberg claims that the oldest meaning of θέμις, almost impossible to trace in Homer, since it had been formed long before both epics came into existence, is connected with religion, or, speaking more accurately, with its form, that it is believed to have at the very beginning.[7] Furthermore, he provides us with a complete analysis of the cult of the deity[8], Themis, whose significance and role in the world religious rite seems to be different than that described in the poetry. It is proved that Themis belonged to the circle of chtonic gods and at the beginning she was very close to, if not totally identical with, Mother Gaia. On the other hand, her particular task was connected with oracles. The cult of Earth and the old oracle-giving have much in common, as it is the Earth that is the source of oracle. This being so, it came as no surprise that both goddesses used to be worshipped in the same places, like Delphi, where the cult of chtonic deities was established earlier than that of Apollo.[9]

One may come to the conclusion that the name of Themis, the goddess worshipped long before Homeric epics, and the history of the notion θέμις stay apart as it was assumed by V. Ehrenberg.[10] He claims that the word θέμις acquired the meaning of an oracle relatively late, and it was not its only and primary sense.

Scrutinizing the history of the word θέμις, Paul Chantraine notes that it had given a name to the deity.[11] Unfortunately, the solution of that controversy is hardly possible at the moment, when there are no written sources describing the religious rites coming from the centuries before Homer.

In the "Iliad", the goddess appears in two scenes: 15, 87-93 and 20, 4-5. The first time we come across her name is the moment when she meets Hera coming back to Olympus.[12] Among other deities Themis rushes ahead

---

[6] V. E h r e n b e r g, op.cit. , p. 1.

[7] V. E h r e n b e r g, op.cit., p. 21 ff. The traces of such religious beliefs are rare in Homer, but they can be found in Homeric Hymns, e.g. the Hymn to Apollo, which preserved older forms of religious terms. In Ehrenberg's opinion the meaning of θέμις is usually connected with oracles, but it is not completely clear, why this sense of the word should be considered older than the others.

[8] Ibidem, pp. 27-36.

[9] Ibidem, pp. 27-36.

[10] Ibidem, p. 30.

[11] P. C h a n t r a i n e, Dictionnaire éthymologique de la langue grecque, histoire des mots, Paris 1990, pp. 427-428.

[12] Il., 15; 87-95, The Iliad, with translation by A. T. M u r r a y, LOEB, vol. I, pp. 72-73,

ἥ δ' ἄλλους μὲν ἔασε, Θέμιστι δὲ καλλιπαρήσω

to greet the Queen, but it is from her that Zeus' wife accepts a cup of ambrosia and to her she speaks. Hera is angry about her husband's will to humiliate Achaean troops in order to honour Achilles. She is also, like the other gods, forbidden to help the Greeks, who are to suffer progressively greater defeat on the battlefield. She takes the cup and this act becomes the beginning of a banquet.

In the next passage Themis is sent by Zeus to gather other gods for a meeting (Il., 20, 4-5):

Ζεὺς δὲ Θέμιστα κελεύσε θεοὺς ἀγορήνδε καλέσσαι
κρατὸς ἀπ' Οὐλύμποιο πολυπτύχον

But Zeus bade Themis summon the gods to the place of gathering from the brow of many ridged Olympus.[13]

These two places, which could easily be overlooked while reading "Iliad", point at the very sense of Themis and her role in the Greek gods' world. In the first scene, she is the one who begins the feast; it may seem a little surprising that this function, in later tradition performed by one of the male gods or a chosen human, like Ganimedes, is carried out by a female deity.[14] As R. Hirzel points out[15], there is a connection between her role as a goddess of gatherings and her role as a symposiarchos: Themis appears to be the goddess of initiative, she is the one who sets things in motion. Certainly, that does not refer to all sorts of activity, but the symposion in the world of Homeric epics seems to be something more than the time of drinking wine and eating. People dine together not only to entertain themselves and to satiate their appetite, but to talk about various, sometimes considerably serious matters. In the "Iliad" and "Odyssey" a dinner is an obligatory prelude to every important discussion or talk to a stranger-guest.[16] (Later

δέκτο δέπας πρώτη γὰρ ἐναυτίνη ἦλθε θέουσα,
καὶ μιν φωνήσασ᾽ ἔπα πτερόεντα προσηύδα

She on her part let be the others, but took the cup from Themis, of the fair cheeks, for she ran first to meet her, and spoke, and addressed her with winged words.

[13] Transl. A. T. M u r r a y, *op.cit.*, vol. I, pp. 370-371.

[14] In the first book of the "Iliad" it is Hephaestos who pours the liquor into the cups (1, 595-600). It seems that in the "Iliad" there is no particular person responsible for that part of the gathering.

[15] R. H i r z e l, *op.cit.*, pp. 12-14.

[16] That refers mainly to the gathering of few people or to the court, for example: Odysseus, Foinix and Aias sent to Achilles with the mission of reconciliation are first invited to eat together with their host (Il., 9, 197-223). Telemachos and his friend begin to explain the reason of their journey to Nestor after being summoned as guests by the king of Pylos (Od., 3;62-71). Also, according to R.Hirzel, Eustathius comments on Il. 9, 73, in the following

on, when Dionysos became the ruler of human feast, this was no longer appropriate.) Homeric gods are also accustomed to discuss while enjoying their meals, so the presence of Themis, who is to become the goddess of justice and political gatherings, is not as surprising, as it seemed to be at the first moment.

The second mentioned passage brings us closer to the main task of Themis, who this time summons other gods to a debate. Doing this she is not acting on her own, but obeying the order of Zeus. He uses her as a messenger, as he does it with Iris or Hermes. The difference lays in the aim of the mission. Themis calls the immortals to the debate, she is not passing the will of the mightiest king. In the "Iliad", there is still no clear mention implying that she is the adviser to the gods.[17] Thus, we may conclude that Homer did not bother to draw our attention to the chtonic cult of the deity. However, we are not in the position to decide whether he did not know it or, which seems a little more probable, he did not need it. All that makes us prone to observe that Themis as a deity in the "Iliad" is rather an insignificant personage.

In the "Odyssey" her name appears only once, in the second book (2, 68-69), when Telemachus calls the names of Zeus and Themis while speaking at the assembly and asking the wooers of Penelope to leave him and his house in peace. Odysseus' son bags, but also warns the people of the wrath of the gods, who punish evil deeds. He strengthens his speech by adding the particular names:

λίσσομαι ἠμὲν Ζηνὸς Ολυμπίου ἠδὲ Θέμιστος
ἥ τ' ἀνδρῶν ἀγορὰς ἠμὲν λύει ἠδὲ καθίζει.

I pray you by Olympian Zeus, and by Themis who looses and gathers the

---

way: καὶ ὅρα ὅπως τὰ ἡρώων ἀεὶ συμπόσια σπουδαῖα ἦσαν, ὡς μυριαχοῦ δηλοῦσιν οἱ σοφοί, οἳ συναφόμενοι τὰ σπουδῆς ἄξια παρ' οἶνον ἐβούλευον. (E u s t a t h i u s P h i l o l o g u s, *Commentarii ad Homeri Iliaem*, vol. 6, 663,7).

[17] Her primary role as the adviser, Ratgeber, to the Olympian gods, and to Zeus in the first place, was fully described by R. H i r z e l (*op.cit.*, pp. 2-7), although his analysis is based also on later literature. He stresses the importance of Themis, whose advice is usually put into practice by the king of gods, so it is possible to draw a conclusion that they, in fact, express the will of Zeus. Themis becomes βουλὴ Διός. By Pindar she is called εὔβουλος (Isth.8, 32; Ol. 13, 8). It is reasonable to add that this has nothing to do with morality. The very good example of her activity is the scene described by the poet of Kypria (Proklos Chretom., Kinkel frg.ep.gr.17), when Thetis advises Zeus to begin a war so as to lighten the burden of the Earth, too crowded with people. R. Hirzel referring to this fragment (op.cit., p. 4) stresses the fact that human beings have not committed any other crime except for being too numerous.

assemblies of men.[18]

In this line, for the first time in poetry, we have the particular role of the goddess described. The epithet is by no means a mere meaningless ornament, as the name of Themis appears so rarely in the text, we cannot say that it is purely formulaic. Here again the name of the goddess stands together with ἀγορά.[19] Furthermore, while in the "Iliad" Themis only summoned gods to the gathering, here we are convinced that she plays a much more important role. Her power refers to the mortals as well, and from Telemachus' words we may infer that by those days it was by well recognised by men. The fact that the name of Themis was linked up with the name of Zeus also proves that the place of that goddess was slightly higher than it used to be in the "Iliad".[20] No moral significance is mentioned in the line quoted above *expressis verbis*, but the lines before it speak about the punishment for men's ill doings, the gods. The who are supposed to execute the punishment are not called by names and the first names appearing in the next line are these of Zeus and Themis, although there is no direct transition from the first sentence to the next and by no means can Themis be associated with the name of a guardian of righteousness. Themis just initiates and finishes gatherings, she is the one who calls them, and not yet the one who cares for the moral aspect of the decisions taken during the meetings. However, it allows us to presume that it may be the beginning of the process, to be fully completed in tragedy, of formation of Themis' new and exceptional image as the goddess of law and order.[21]

Having briefly analysed the position of Themis in both epics, we may proceed to the notion much more frequent and important in Homeric world: θέμις, and its plural form: θέμιστες. The relation between the name of the deity and the noun is not entirely clear or satisfactorily explained. As I have already mentioned[22], it is still a matter of some dispute. For the time being, we will put it aside and try to demonstrate how significant a role the term θέμις played in the society described by Homer. We shall partly follow

---

[18] transl. A.T. M u r r a y, *The Odyssey*, LOEB, 1965, vol. I, p. 70.

[19] The altars of Themis were situated in the place of meetings.

[20] Certainly it may be due to the fact that each of the epics describes Olympian gods differently; in the "Iliad" general, the immortals look more human-like, whereas in the "Odyssey" they assume a certain grade of superhuman dignity.

[21] V. E h r e n b e r g (*op.cit.*, pp. 40-41) persuades that till quite a late period Themis was not the goddess of law and describing her function this way is just an overstatement or a pure misunderstanding. Themis as a chtonic deity belonging to the world of Tytans appeared in Hesiod. This was also Hesiod who bound her name with justice.

[22] see ref. 1.

the opinion of V. Ehrenberg, for whom the meaning of θέμις was in the first place connected with the life of society, later πόλις. It is not the principle of an individual's behaviour, having or not having anything to do with his relationships with other individuals; on the contrary, it seems quite clear that it is in the middle of social life and touches the most important aspects of the well-being of a community.

In both poems θέμις in such meaning appears quite often. However, it is not possible to reduce this complex term to one, clear sense. This kind of reduction may be and is performed in the surveys whose authors, referring to longer period, have to point out only the most important and the most characteristic definition of θέμις[23], or rather of θέμιστες. The plural form occurs in the "Iliad" six times.[24] First and foremost, θέμιστες are inseparably connected with kingship.

In the words of Odysseus, we find the shortest and perhaps the most striking theory of power and its role in the social order. While trying to stop Achaean soldiers rushing back to the ships, in order to restore peace, he expresses the basic opinion defining social roles of different sorts of men:

Il. 2, 204-206
οὐκ ἀγαθὸν πολυκοιρανίη· εἷς κοίρανος ἔστω,
εἷς βασιλεύς, ᾧ δῶκε Κρόνου πάϊς ἀγκυλομήτεω
σκῆπτρόν τ᾽ ἠδὲ θέμιστας, ἵνά σφισι βουλεύῃσι.

Let there be one lord, one king, to whom the son of crooked-counselling Cronos hath vouchsaved the sceptre and judgements, that he may take council for his people.[25]

The very same words are repeated by Nestor, who addresses Agamemnon in the ninth book:

Il., 9, 96 - 99
Ἀτρείδη κύδιστε ἄναξ ἀνδρῶν Ἀγάμεμνον

---

[23] See, for example: J. W. J o n e s, *The Law and Legal Theory of the Greeks*, Oxford 1956, G. G l o t z, *La cité grecque,*Paris1988 (first published: Paris1928), K. R a a f l a u b, *Die Anfange des politischen Denkens bei den Griechen.* in: *Pipers Handbuch der politischen Ideen,* ed. I.Fischer & H.Muncher, B.I, *Fruhe Hochkulturen und europäische Antike,* Munchen - Zurich 1988.

[24] Il., 1.238; 2, 206; 9. 99; 9. 156; 9. 298; 16. 387.

[25] transl. A.T. M u r r a y, *op.cit.,* p. 65; German translation: *einer soll Herr sein, einer Konig, dem der sohn des krummgesonnenen Kronos Stab und Satzungen gab, dass er Konig sei unter ihnen,* W. S c h a d e w a l d t s, *Neue Ubertragung Homers Ilias,* Baden-Baden 1988.

ἐν σοὶ μὲν λήξω, σέο δ' ἄρξομαι, οὕνεκα πολλῶν
λαῶν ἐσσι ἄναξ καί τοι Ζεὺς ἐγγυάλιξε
σκῆπτρόν τ' ἠδὲ θέμιστας, ἵνά σφισι βουλεύησθα.

Most glorious son of Atreus, Agamemnon, king of men, with thee will I begin and with the make an end, for that thou art king over many hosts, and to thee Zeus hath vouchsafed the sceptre and judgments, that thou mayest take council for thy people.[26]

In the remainder of his speech, Nestor reminds the honoured ruler of his great mistakes, which caused the departure of Achilles disastrous for the whole Greek army. His remark that as a king Agamemnon should speak first at the assembly, but is also obliged to listen to the advice of other people, must sound very bitter at the moment. Nestor also repeats his counsel as to the way of bringing the offended hero back to the battle filed. Agamemnon agrees with all the accusations, but is prone to share the responsibility with Ate, the Madness, sent to him by Zeus. It seems obvious that Nestor does not admire Agamemnon as a man. What he honours and to what he pays his deepest respect is the position of the ruler, his wealth and, most important, the special character of his power. In the first nine books of the "Iliad" we have been given proofs to understand that Agamemnon himself is not the best, the bravest or the wisest of the Greeks. His stubbornness, greed and reluctance to accept good advice jeopardized not only the victory, but even the safety of the Greek army. What is more, everybody seems to know this and, despite it, the king of Mycenae keeps his position and preserves his power over the troops and their leaders. There is only one logical explanation, and it is given in two passages quoted above. Odysseus' words form a general statement and, as it were, describe the facts. The power of kings comes straight from Zeus, who, being a king himself, stands for a source of the mortal rulers' authority.

The exceptional authority of Agamemnon is based on the particular sceptre he possesses. The son of Cronos gave the king his sceptre, the symbol of power and judgements. The significance of this combination has been pointed out by many scholars.[27]

The sceptre itself plays not the slightest role. We are told its history and its meaning cannot be limited to that of a symbol.[28]

---

[26] Transl. A.T.M u r r a y, *op.cit.*, p. 389.

[27] Among others: V. E h r e n b e r g, *op.cit.*, pp.4-5, G. G l o t z, *op.cit.*, p. 48, K. R a a-f l a u b, *op.cit.*, p. 196, R. H i r z e l.

[28] Kings are called σκηπτοῦχοι, (Il. 1. 86; 274); the sceptre of Agamemnon was produced by Hephaestos for Zeus, who gave it by Hermes to Pelops and his children. The whole

What does the term "judgements" mean? We cannot speak about the laws yet. A king is supposed to make decisions and his decisions have, as G. Glotz expressed it, supernatural inspiration, that enables them to meet any problems, especially to restore peace among his subjects.[29] Later, in the "Odyssey", the authority of this term defining the king's decisions will be strengthened by using it to designate the will of Zeus: θέμιστες Διός.[30] By this time, what we have is the assumption that a king makes his decisions with some sort of divine help and he does so in order to advice his people. Ergo: his exceptional potential was not given to him by mere chance or even because of his celebrated ancestors; we do not know whether all the decisions taken by a king can de called θέμιστες, it is rather doubtful. He exercises this power only as a master and a councillor of his people to ensure them successful and peaceful existence.

On the other hand, the words of the king resemble the expression of divine will. They should be obeyed and put into practice without further discussion.[31] In war-time a king of Agamemnon's position possesses the highest power as the chief commander.[32]

---

history and power of this family, its connections with the immortals, is closed in that piece of wood. In other places in Homeric epics we were shown the way the "ordinary" sceptre is used: e.g. in the "Odyssey", the sceptre is passed by the herald to the speaker at the meeting as a sign of permission to begin a speech (Od. 2. 37-38).

[29] G. G l o t z, op.cit., p. 53: "Avec le sceptre, il (le roi) a reçu la connaissance des θέμιστες, ces inspirations surnaturelles qui permettent d'aplanir toutes des difficultés et, spécialement, de rétablir la paix intérieure par les paroles de justice".

[30] Od., 16, 403.

[31] G. G l o t z, op.cit., pp. 52-53, underlines the power of a king by stressing that he is a highest priest as wll: "Mediateur des hommes auprès des dieux, le roi est aussi le représentant des dieux parmi les hommes".

[32] G. Glotz claims that Agamemnon, as a chief commander was able to sentence a man to death without any formal procedure, (op.cit., p. 53); to prove this statement he reminds the passage from the second book of the "Iliad", (2. 391 sqq.) and Aristotle interpretation of these lines:

ὃν δέ κ' ἐγὼν ἀπάνευθε μάχης ἐθέλοντα νοήσω
μιμνάζειν παρὰ νηυσὰ κορωνίσιν, οὔ οἱ ἔπειτα
ἄρκιον ἐσσεῖται φυγέειν κύνας ἠδ' οἰωνούς.

Agamemnon is trying the courage of his army; he tells them to prepare to the battle and warns against behaving cowardly. His words cannot be understood as the expressis verbis execution of the king's privilege; there are no other passages, that could make it certain, but this doubt can be applied to most of Homeric customs and "rights". Aristotle interprets it as the right that the king had only during the campaign, and not, for instance, at the meeting, where the king had to stand even critical remarks of his subjects (Polit., 1285a). As a matter of fact, there is too little evidence to be sure, how this prerogative worked. There is no incident showing its power in the real life. One seems to be certain: a Homeric

Till this moment everything seems clear and straightforward. The problem emerges, however, when one tries to compare this pattern with the action of the "Iliad". The first thing that comes to one's mind is that the decisions of a king are not necessarily right. Agamemnon does not have to consult his decisions with the rest of the army, although it is better to take their opinion into consideration, and one should remember that in the "Iliad" the opinion of the army means the opinion expressed by the leaders.[33] He is wrong, even if the responsibility is to be shared by the gods. Still, the question remains whether we are allowed to call his further decision θέμις or not. Perhaps that does not refer to this particular situation, where the matter involves the king himself. He does not decide about his subjects, we are tempted to say: he cannot be impartial. Analyzing the meaning of θέμιστες[34] R. Hirzel begins it with the phrase from the "Odyssey" mentioned above, where θέμιστες Διός are just the expression of the divine will.

---

king, who was also the commander of other minor βασιλεῖς, had probably more power than the others ruler; it must have applied to the capital punishment as well, however, to whom we do not know and under what circumstances it could be used. The words of Agamemnon could just show his temper. On the other hand, all the customs and "laws" obeyed by the Homeric society belong to the sphere of unwritten rules, which, when generally accepted or imposed, made someone's power strong and solid.

[33] In his interesting, but not always right (in our opinion) analysis of the political thinking in Homeric epics, K. Raaflaub stresses very much the fact of the critic addressed to Agamemnon in the first and second book of the "Iliad" (K. R a a f l a u b, op.cit., pp. 205-211). In these scenes he sees the beginning of the process leading to the expansion of the power of the people. Basically it is right, but the picture drawn by this scholar seems to be fragmentary. The critic of the kings and the aristocracy can certainly be found in Homer, even in the "Iliad", but it is only a very small part of the poem, which, as a whole, brings the glorification of the aristocratic society. The most violent attack towards the noble leaders is presented by Thersites, whose pathetic appearance is mocked by everybody. His words, in the opinion of every modern reader are true, but they, as well as the speaker, are rejected by the army, by the ordinary soldiers. The next problem is connected with the role of the meeting of the army. Such a meeting is called, whenever important decisions are to be taken, the presence of all the soldiers is perhaps necessary and, theoretically, everybody is allowed to speak. However, the only not aristocratic speaker appears to be Thersites. He is rebuked and bitten by Odysseus, who gains the applause of the soldiers. The importance of the meeting probably consists in its mere presence. And M. Gagarin is close to the truth, when he points out the presence of the people in the analysis of the legal procedures in Homer. (M. G a g a r i n, *Early Greek Law,* Berkeley-Los Angeles-London 1986). It seems to be reasonable to accept, that the public witnessing the decision being taken made it valid. The most important events, decisions, oaths and words should be said in the public, the presence of which is crucial to the Homeric men. Still, the presence of the people is the silent presence, the background for the actions of the heroes, who need it to exist. Yet, in the "Iliad" we cannot speak about any real political power connected with it.

[34] R. H i r z e l, *op.cit.,* pp. 24-25.

On these grounds he compares the significance of the mortal king's judgement with the superhuman and practically unlimited power of the Olympians.[35] However, this conclusion seems to be a little too hasty. Never in the "Iliad" is the word θέμις referred to the will of Zeus. We should not support our interpretation by the later text. In the first Homeric epic θέμιστες are king's judgements, that means: decisions of a higher authority, not being subject to discussion. (The word "judgement" does not signify the legal process, since in the "Iliad" the king's decisions are not clearly connected with disputes between the parties.) The dispute can take place earlier, but the final decision belongs to the king, who, obviously, can take the advice into consideration.[36] His words are not a legal act or a decree, nor are they of general character. They concern a particular matter, as it is shown in several places in the epic. On the other hand, R.Hirzel is right, when he emphasizes the fact, that a king possesses the wisdom, which was given to him and which tells him what to do. This wisdom is the most essential element of his authority.[37] What might be added, is that it concerns the ideal state of affairs and an ideal ruler. Nonetheless, no matter what the quality of a man being a king is, his θέμιστες preserve their power.

For R. Hirzel[38] the θέμιστες of a king play the same role in the community of men as the orders of Zeus play in the world. They are in fact the measure by which the highest god expresses his will to human beings. And this makes them very close to the oracles.

V. Ehrenberg emphasizes the connection between θέμιστες, which are believed to be one of the most important symbols of kingship, and βούλαι.[39] He does not hesitate to speak about the sanctity of the king's power; that way a king becomes Zeus' representative on the Earth. This is a decisive factor in his τιμή. Moreover, it is not a coincidence that Agamemnon's daughter mentioned in the "Iliad" is called Χρυσόθεμις.[40] The king, called by V. Ehrenberg the incarnation of a god[41], is also able to have counsels (βούλεσθαι) not like an ordinary man.

---

[35] Certainly the power of Zeus in the Homeric epics seems to be limited by Moira, but we are told that Zeus is able to change the lot (for instance: Il. 16, 439-445). Perhaps the will of Zeus is the strongest, when it goes hand in hand with Moira, as suggests A. K r o- k i e w i c z, *Moralność Homera i etyka Hezjoda,* Warszawa 1959, pp. 73-96.

[36] K. Raaflaub presumes, on the other hand, that θέμιστες were also obligatory for the king; they were the way of controlling and criticizing of the ruler, *op.cit.*, p. 212.

[37] R. H i r z e l, *op.cit.*, pp. 23-25, the same: G. G l o t z, *op.cit.*, pp. 51-57.

[38] *Ibidem.*

[39] V. E h r e n b e r g, *op.cit.*, p. 4.

[40] Il. 9. 145; 287.

[41] V. E h r e n b e r g, *op.cit.*, p. 7.

Bearing in mind the importance and particular character of king's θέμιστες one may be a little surprised that a ruler is not the only source of such decisions.

In the "Iliad" 1, 238-239 we grasp a short remark that can give us a clue:

νῦν αὖτέ μιν υἶες 'Αχαιῶν
ἐν παλάμῃς φορέουσι δικασπόλοι, οἵ τε θέμιστας
πρὸς Διὸς εἰρύαται;

now the sons of Achaeans that give judgements bear it (the sceptre) in their hands.[42]

Taking his oath in the first book, Achilles tells us about the procedure performed by δικασπόλοι - judges, who, sceptre as a symbol of their authority in hand, give their decisions. This seems to mean that at this stage, the society already had the possibility to take care of disputes. At all probability, a king still was the most natural and the first institution to whom litigants turned in order to settle their quarrel, but it was already shown in the previous chapter, covering the famous scene from the shield of Achilles, that the legal procedure was developed to a recognizable degree.[43] The same is suggested by even more important passage, already analysed in the previous chapter,[44] the impressive simile of the tempest devastating everything, when Zeus is raging against men "that by violence give crooked judgements in the place of gathering wrecking not of the vengeance of the gods"[45]

- οἳ βίῃ εἰν ἀγορῇ σκολιὰς κρίνωσι θέμιστας,
ἐκ δὲ δίκην ἐλάσωσι θεῶν ὄπιν οὐκ ἀλέγοντες;

Together with the fragment listed above, these lines let us draw an image of a certain procedure connected with θέμιστες. They are issued by some higher authority, let it be a king or δικαπόλοι (in that option we deal probably with a collegial body consisting of older men), during public meeting, as it may be inferred from the text (εἰν ἀγορῇ)[46], and while giving their decision the judges bear the sceptre. Their decisions, however, are not necessarily right, although there are no criteria, like written rules, that can be objective terms of reference. It seems that they are estimated according to

[42] Transl. A.T.M u r r a y, *op.cit.*, p. 21.
[43] See the analysis of M. G a g a r i n, *op.cit.*, p.7 ff.
[44] Ssee "Δίκη in the "Iliad".
[45] Il. 16. 387-388, transl. A.T. M u r r a y, *op.cit.*, p. 193.
[46] That brings us back to the goddess Themis, whose relation to the ἀγορά was already stressed.

common beliefs, or rather conventional norms and, perhaps, according to personal convictions of the two sides in the dispute.

On the other hand, it is clearly stated that "crooked judgements" are going to be the reason of divine wrath. It is difficult to define the criteria of this sanction; at least it is to be remembered that there is always hope for people being judged by δικαπόλοι; in the case, when the verdict is not a satisfactory one, they can expect divine punishment over the wrong judges.

This allows us to assume that here for the first time we meet some moral qualification connected with θέμιστες. They are no longer arbitrary decisions of men of power. These men are not unpunished, if not their subjects or fellow citizens, it is a deity that will judge their work.

In the "Iliad", 11, 806-809 we are exactly told where the judgements and decisions were taken:

ἀλλ᾽ ὅτε δὴ κατὰ νῆας ᾽Οδυσσῆος θείοιο
ἷξε θέων Πάτροκλος, ἵνά σφ᾽ ἀγορή τε θέμις τε
ἤην, τῇ δὴ καί σφι θεῶν ἐτετεύχατο βωμοί,

But when in his running Patroclus was come to the ships of godlike Odysseus, where was their place of gathering and the giving of dooms, whereby also were builded their altars of the gods.[47]

Here again we have got something that resembles the centre of the community's life: ἀγορή and together with it θέμις, the term here designates the place where θέμις - a doom or judgement - was made. As it was pointed out above, such a connection sends us to the deity, whose relationship with gatherings seems to begin to be clear in the "Iliad". In the vicinity of the administrative power we see the oldest place of religious cult:[48] the altar of the gods. That binds together three aspects of city life (in the "Iliad" the life of a camp, which is organized in a way resembling a city):

- religion giving sanction to the rest
- gathering - decision -making, the place where all the important businesses of the state and its community were discussed,
- settlement of disputes.

V. Ehrenberg[49] claims that this connection has probably not too long a tradition, since in the Mycenaean monarchy it was the palace of the king that played the role of a centre. In the "Iliad" it would be compared to the exceptional significance of Agamemnon's tent. Nevertheless, the aristoc-

---

[47] Transl. A.T. M u r r a y, *op.cit.*, p. 541.
[48] R. H i r z e l, *op.cit.*, pp. 9-10.
[49] V. E h r e n b e r g, *op.cit.*, p. 12.

racy found it natural and necessary to be able to talk about public matters.[50]
It seems to be obvious that this combination ἀγορή - θέμις - βωμοί is the
prophecy for the future, even if the crucial decisions were eventually taken
by a monarch, it must have been done in public.

For V. Ehrenberg θέμις in that place belongs inseparably to the aristocratic code and creates one of its most important factors; "Keine θέμις ist
denkbar ohne ἀγορή wie umgekehrt keine ἀγορή ohne θέμις".[51] This statement, drawing a very clear and simple image of social organisation of Homeric society, sounds however a little too decisive, too categorical and too
dogmatic. At this stage of the social development and with the "Iliad" as a
source we do not possess enough material to prove it.

Before going further towards another, slightly different meaning of θέμις,
we should have a closer look upon the line which, binding θέμιστες with
the prerogatives of a king, cannot be placed together with the earlier examples.

Agamemnon, while trying to persuade Achilles to come back to fight,
promises to the insulted hero several donations and the hand of his daughter, with her rich dowry Achilles would be a king of many cities, where

ἐν δ' ἄνδρες ναίουσι πολύρρηνες πολυβοῦται,
οἵ κέ ἑ δωτίνῃσι θεὸν ὣς τιμήσουσι
καί οἱ ὑπὸ σκήπτρῳ λιπαρὰς τελέουσι θέμιστας.[52]

A. T. Murray translated this passage as follows:[53]
In them dwell men rich in flocks and rich in kine
men that shall honour him (scl. Achilles) with gifts
as though he were a god, and beneath his sceptre shall bring
his ordinances to prosperous fulfilment.

It is clear that A. T. Murray omitted the difficulty presented by the phrase
λιπαρὰς θέμιστας by changing the order of the words; he treated the adjective λιπαρός as an adverb depicting the verb τελέουσι. The epithet λιπαρός,
however, sounds in that context a little astonishing and attracts our attention. Λιπαρός meaning: oily, shiny, prosperous, brilliant, in an attributive

---

[50] For complex analysis see: S. P a r n i c k i - P u d e ł k o, *Agora. Geneza i rozwój
rynku greckiego,* Warszawa – Wrocław 1957; especially the second chapter (pp. 38-49)
provides the description of the *agora* in the archaic Greece; the survey based mainly on the
archaeological data comprises the literary evidence as well.

[51] V. E h r e n b e r g, *op.cit.,* p. 12.

[52] Il., 9. 154-156; 296-298.

[53] A.T. M u r r a y, *op.cit.,* pp. 398, 403.

position to the θέμιστες was always discussed and A.T. Murray's translation is not the only possible interpretation.

The authors of the Great Greek-English Lexicon[54] translated θέμιστες as "tribute". The German translation by W. Schadewaldts[55] is much more literal:

und Männerwohnen darin, reich an Herden, reich an Rindern,
Die mit Beschenkungen wie einen Gott ihn ehren werden
Und unter seinem Herrscherstab ihm fette Satzungen erfüllen.

The Liddel-Scott version, in our opinion, is not plausible; we follow A. T. Murray, V. Ehrenberg[56] and W. Schadewaldts, according to whom θέμιστες here denote king's decisions, ordinances, which, if brought into fulfilment (τελεῖν) by eager subjects, might turn to be "oily", which means bringing fat and wealth, profitable.

R. Hirzel expresses more or less the same opinion translating the phrase: "*gewinnenbringende Ermahnungen*".[57] The difference consists in the word "Ermahnungen", admonitions. The role of a king, according to this interpretation, is connected with admonishing, warning his subjects. His better knowledge lets him warn them against wrong choices. On the other hand, that would limit the royal authority to a negative role and it seems reasonable to accept, that the king is also supposed to give positive advice to the people.

What is really remarkable in these lines is the comparison of a king to the god (ὡς θεόν). The sceptre, the symbol of power and authority, in the hand of a ruler resembles a magic wand whose movement was able to make dreams come true.

The profit of θέμιστες belongs not necessarily to the king only. Like a god who rules mortals and provides them with what they need, a mortal king is able to make the lives of his subjects happy; although we may only guess to what extent he cares about it.

In all other passages in the "Iliad", θέμις appears only in the singular. This separates it from all the instances analysed above (ἀγορή τε θέμις τε as well). It looses its clearly concrete meaning and lets us look for a more abstract sense.

Most appearances of θέμις in the older Homeric epic seem to be at least slightly formalised and have the form of a phrase, which may introduce a genitive or dative case as a noun and a verb as a predicate. Almost none of

---

[54] *The Great Greek-English Lexicon, compiled by H.G. Liddel &R. Scott, revised by H.S. Jones*, Oxford 1940 (1973).

[55] W. Schadewaldts, Homer *Ilias*, Frankfurt am Main 1988, p. 143.

[56] V. Ehrenberg, *op.cit.*, p. 8.

[57] R. Hirzel, *op.cit.*, p. 39.

these instances of θέμις is completely clear and unmistakable. Generally, it may be claimed that θέμις usually describes a sort of a norm of behaviour that is either established by higher will or, which is more common, by custom.

The first meaning, expression of divine will or commandment, what is sometimes considered to be the most important sense of θέμις, in the "Iliad" occurs rarely. It is necessary to stress once more that θέμις is not an abstract term corresponding to the name of the goddess.[58]

R. Hirzel tends to find the meaning of an advice in almost all cases[59], he emphasizes this sense of θέμις in the noun and in the name of the deity as well. However, one must remember that his analysis is not a diachronic one, it is based on different works and gives the complete picture of the term with little consideration for the historical development of the notion. The significance of advice as the most important element in the sense of the term is due to the fact that he describes Themis as the goddess of oracles, i. e., the deity who passes to the people the will of gods. The same can be said about the θέμιστες of mortal men; they can be also treated as the expression of the will of someone, who knows better and whose opinion should be accepted as a good piece of advice.

Such an interpretation, though interesting, seems to be very one-sided and subjective.

For V. Ehrenberg[60] the fact that θέμις has so many different senses and in some of them had become a formulaic expression already in the "Iliad", proves, that by the time the first poem was composed θέμις had already had a long history. In addition, the roots of this term must be traced back to the circle of primitive beliefs. A trace of such understanding of θέμις we may find in the "Iliad", 16, 793 - 797, in the dramatic scene of the Patroclos' death:

τοῦ δ' ἀπὸ μὲν κρατὸς κυνέην βάλε Φοῖβος Ἀπόλλων;
ἡ δὲ κυλινδομένη καναχὴν ἔχε ποσσὶν ὑφ' ἵππων

---

[58] R. H i r z e l suggests (op.cit., p. 8) that the primary significance of θέμις was already forgotten since what we have in Homer, is the concrete and meaning full of life. The dispute what should be considered older: θέμις or Θέμις is still open and we do not think that any proof solving this controversy could ever emerge. What we can do is the analysis of the term's meaning and conclusion that most places there is no distinct connection with the name of the deity. Both names had probably existed much earlier, before Homeric epics were composed, and it could be reasonable to claim that the division took place in this earlier period. On the other hand, the process of uniting the name of the deity with the meaning of the noun is to be seen again in the next epic, in the "Odyssey".

[59] R. H i r z e l, op.cit., p. 41.

[60] V. E h r e n b e r g, op.cit., pp. 5-7.

αὐλῶπις τρυφάλεια, μιάνθησαν δὲ ἔθειραι
αἵματι καὶ κονίῃσι; πάρος γε μὲν οὐ θέμις ἦεν
ἱππόκομον πήληκα μιαίνεσθαι κονίῃσιν,
ἀλλ' ἀνδρὸς θείοιο κάρη χαρίεν τε μέτωπον
ῥύετ' 'Αχιλλῆος; τότε δὲ Ζεὺς "Εκτορι δῶκεν
ᾗ κεφαλῇ φορέειν, σχεδόθεν δέ οἱ ἦεν ὄλεθρος.

And from his head Phoebus Apollo smote the helmet that
rang a sit rolled beneath the feet of the horses, the crested helm;
and the plumes were befoulrd with blood and dust.
Not until that hour had the gods suffered that helm with plume
of horse-hair to be befouled with dust, but ever did it guard
the head and the comely brow of a godlike man, even of Achilles:
but then Zeus youchsafed it to Hector, to wear upon his head,
yet was destruction near at hand for him.[61]

As this translation clearly suggests θέμις is the gods' will. Exactly it is Apollo who represents this higher power. And this power regards even such a "normal" and everyday matter as falling down of an object. It was not possible that the helmet that Patroclus wore could fall down of the knight's head before it was permitted by the god. Otherwise οὐ θέμις ἦεν.[62] Certainly, the divine intervention is not in the first place limited to such a trivial sphere. On the contrary, this incident illustrates the might of the immortals; even such a simple fact can depend on the divine decision. It can refer to all events in human life indiscriminately and it is the god who decides, whether or not his will should be expressed in a more distinct way in a particular case. In addition, it is quite obvious that here the moment when gods let the Patroclus' helmet fall down, signifies the end of the young man's life.

Before, he almost managed to change Moira's order and was close to capture Troy (Il. 16, 707-708):

οὔ νύ τοι αἶσα
σῷ ὑπὸ δουρὶ πόλιν πέρθαι Τρώων ἀγερώχων,

Patroclus' fierce bravery and strength turned out to be irresistible. Had there been no omnipotent gods watching the battle field and decided to interfere, the young knight would have become the conqueror of Troy. Divine cruel intervention and the clandestine attack of Apollo are far from

---

[61] transl. A.T. M u r r a y, *op.cit.*, II, p. 223.
[62] V. E h r e n b e r g, *op.cit.*, pp. 6-8.

being an example of honourable behaviour.[63]

Θέμις appears here as a negation, a sort of prohibition: οὐ θέμις ἦεν - it was not permitted, and θέμις itself denotes gods' will, Gebot Gottes. V. Ehrenberg interpreting this passage claims that θέμις must have come from the past and belonged to the sphere of the very primitive imagination that used to explain every single fact by a divine action,[64] the divine will which cannot be broken by mere mortals. Such behaviour would be οὐ θέμις. We come across the very similar expression in Il. 14, 386-387, when Poseidon himself joins the battle; however, it is not θέμις for the people to fight with a deity:

τῷ δ' οὐ θέμις ἐστὶ μιγῆναι
ἐν δαῖ λευγαλέῃ, ἀλλὰ δέος ἰσχάνει ἄνδρας.

Where it is not permitted that any should mingle in dreadful war, but terror holds men aloof therefrom.[65]

The basic conclusion driven from both these passages must be that θέμις of gods refers to a definite situation and does not create any coherent set of rules (this makes it similar to the θέμις of the mortal kings). In many other

---

[63] The death of Patroclos seems to be particular and too awful even as compared to the rest of the "Iliad" (see: *The Iliad; A Commentary* ed. G. S. K i r k, R. J a n k o, vol. IV, Cambridge 1992). G. S. Kirk begins his interpretation of this scene with the series of questions referring to the sense of the sinister action of Apollo. The hero must be deprived of Achilles' armour, which is impenetrable, otherwise he cannot be killed. The fact, that it is done by a deity himself, in a way honours Patroclus' bravery. On the other hand, the whole scene came under suspicion, for it was not understandable, why Homer deprived Hector of the glory of killing the Achaian hero and let the first hit to a completely unknown personality, Euphorbos. Some scholar believe this scene replaced another, where Hector slew Patroclos alone.

The question of the armour has also long been a matter of dispute; Edwords (H.P. 264) claims that Patroclos not being of immortal γένος should not use the equipment made for a son of a goddess. He appeared to be helpless in the face of Apollo. The fallen helmet symbolizes the head of a hero, that is going to fallow it to lay in the dust. It is also not clear, in what moment Patroclos turns back to Euphorbos.

In our opinion even more important doubts are implied by the general meaning of this passage and its connection with Moira, Aisa; if the lot of Troy is already made and it is not Patroclos who is going to destroy the town, how it is at all possible that he almost takes the city? Can we infer from the text that without Apollo Troy would have been captured not by the right person? It seems a little illogical that the Destiny needs some help to came into being; or perhaps we should treat Apollo as a part of Moira?

No matter how many details should stay unexplained the bottom line is that the scene of the death of Patroclos predicts the death of Hector and the end of Achilles.

[64] V. E h r e n b e r g, *op.cit.*, pp. 6-8.

[65] Transl. A. T. M u r r a y, *op.cit.*, II, p. 95.

situations men were killed and although it should be presumed that it happened not against divine doom, it did not necessarily involve supernatural assistance. Moreover, both Greek and Trojan knights used to fight immortal enemies and were even able to harm them, like Diomedes who scratched Ares and Aphrodite.[66] Nowhere did it happen against θέμις.

Now we may proceed to the θέμις which begins to arrange the life of a community as well as that of a single human being. This θέμις approaches a rule, still not codified, not written, partly applied just in a concrete case, but very important, since it becomes the factor denoting what is right, what is fitting. In other words it defines the common feeling as to what can be done without any harm or what should be done as being expected.

The first place where this occurs in the text is the "Iliad" 2, 72-74; Agamemnon is going to try his army and he proposes to come back home. This rather surprising test was not suggested to the king by the dream sent by Zeus in order to make the Achaean troops suffer.

> ἀλλ' ἄγετ' αἴ κέν πως θωρήξομεν υἷας 'Αχαιῶν;
> πρῶτα δ' ἐγὼν ἔπεσιν πειρήσομαι, ἦ θέμις ἐστί,
> καὶ φεύγειν σὺν νηυσὶ πολυκλήϊσι κελεύσω;

Nay, come now, if in any wise we may, let us arm the sons of Achaeans; but first will I make trial of them in speech, as it is right, and will bid them flee with their benched ships.[67]

It has been suggested in a recent analysis provided by G. S. Kirk[68] that the expression ἦ θέμις ἐστί added by Agamemnon most probably refers to the custom, not to his prerogatives as a commander; it may have been added in order to appease any sort of surprise or opposition of other commanders who constituted a council. G. S. Kirk assumes that by that time θέμις ἐστί was a formulaic expression that could cover an unexpected or odd sequence of words or ideas.[69] Designating proper behaviour or ritual it comes regularly at the beginning or at the end of a verse.[70] According to V. Ehrenberg, who expresses a completely different opinion[71], θέμις in the "Iliad" 2, 72-74 represents the personal will and it can be understood neither as a decision (Satzung), rule, nor as a custom, law of nature or advice. We cannot

---

[66] Il., 5. 337 sqq., 855 sqq.

[67] Transl. A. T. M u r r a y, *op.cit.* I, p. 55.

[68] G. S. K i r k, *The Iliad: A Commentary,* Cambridge 1985, vol. I, p. 122.

[69] *Ibidem.*

[70] It proves to be accurate in: Il, 2. 73; 9. 33; 9. 14; 9. 276; 11. 779; 19. 177; 22. 44; 23. 581; 24. 652.

[71] V. E h r e n b e r g, *op.cit.*, pp. 8-9.

follow this statement. Θέμις in this place denotes a sort of behaviour typical or at least expected from a king. It is not this concrete decision of testing the army that is θέμις; θέμις is the possibility, that can be used by a king. He can do such a thing and, here V. Ehrenberg is right, it is only his will that puts it into practice; there is no advice (who and to whom is supposed to give one?). But a king is just using his power, this is permitted, this is fitting, that is, what one could expect, and in that sense it is θέμις.

On the other hand, this concrete decision may be a little odd, it may even prove to be dangerous to the Greeks (and it turns to be so), so the king straightens his words by reminding the other commanders: this is θέμις. Otherwise there would be no need to use this term at all. He would have just given an order. So, the interpretation of G. S. Kirk seems to be more plausible than that given by V. Ehrenberg.

The very same sense of the term θέμις we get in the "Iliad" 9, 32-33. Diomedes, who is the first to speak at the meeting, feels that it would be better if he explained his deed. He has two reasons to think so: he is young and he is going to speak before the elder, and he is going to scold the chief commander, Agamemnon. There can be no doubt that Diomedes has enough reasons to rebuke the Mycenaean king, nevertheless, he stresses that he sticks to the custom:

'Ατρείδη σοὶ πρῶτα μαχήσομαι ἀφραδέοντι,
ἢ θέμις ἐστὶν ἄναξ ἀγορῆ; σὺ δὲ μή τι χολωθῆς.

Son of Atreus, with thee first will I contend in the folly, where it is meet, o king, even in the place of gathering: and be not thou wrath thereat.[72]

The most surprising element in the A. T. Murray's translation is the word "even" suggesting that quarrelling with one's king should be especially rebuked when done in public. This would mean that it would be easier to do it in private. In our opinion the public here is crucial. It has to be done in the place of gathering, in front of the people (here: soldiers).

In the "Iliad" 23, 581 the young and cunning son of Nestor, Antilochus, is told to behave, since it is θέμις:

'Αντίλοχή εἰ δ' ἄγε δεῦρο διοτρεφές, ἢ θέμις ἐστί,
στὰς ἵππων προπάροιθε καὶ ἄρματος, αὐτὰρ ἱμάσθλην
χερσὶν ἔχε ῥαδινήν, ἣ περ τὸ πρόσθεν ἔλαυνες,
ἵππων ἀψάμενος γαιήοχον ἐννοσίγαιον
ὄμνυθι μὴ μὲν ἑκὼν τὸ ἐμὸν δόλῳ ἄρμα πεδῆσαι.

---

[72] Transl. A. T. M u r r a y, *op.cit.* I, p. 385.

Antilochos, fostered of Zeus, up, come thou hither and, as is appointed
way, stand thou before thy horses and chariot, and take in hand the slender
lask (...) and swear by him that holdeth and shaketh the earth that not of
thine own will didst thou hinder my chariot.[73]

Antilochus has just won the chariot race, but he must ascribe his victory
not to the better horses, but to his own cleverness, which showed him how
to cheat Menelaus. As it is obvious to everybody that Menelaus should
have bitten Nestor's son, Antilochus must defend himself in front of the
Greeks. What he should do is θέμις and he is asked to take an oath.[74] That
seems to be a commonly accepted way of proving one's innocence and settling the dispute. A litigant taking an oath is aware of the responsibility
connected with that act; the divine punishment for the false oath must have
been treated as a real factor making people say the truth. Antilochus cannot
avoid it, or rather should respect it, although there is no written rule order-
ing him to do what Menelaus asks him to.(As a matter of fact he is not able
to swear his innocence and he prefers to give back his award in order not to
take an oath, that would be true, but not profitable, or false, but connected
with a danger of future punishment.) Nevertheless it is θέμις. Murray's translation of θέμις in that passage as "an appointed way" only partly expresses
the sense of this term. As V. Ehrenberg claims[75] θέμις cannot be translated
straight-forward as a rule or a custom, although it has much in common
with these two notions. It constitutes sort of a norm, ruling the life of a
society, and as it is obvious in the "Iliad", the society of noblemen, whose
lives should be subjected to this order, known to everybody and commonly
understood. If one's behaviour can be judged as decent, meet, that means
within the accepted boundaries, it can be described as being in accord with
θέμις.[76]

---

[73] *Ibidem,* II, p. 537.

[74] The role of the oath in settling a dispute has long been discussed; see: R. H i r z e l,
Der Eid, Aalen 1966, M. G a g a r i n, *Early Greek Law,* Berkeley-Los Angeles-London
1986, G. T h ü r, *Oaths and Dispute Settlement in Ancient Greek Law,* in: *Greek Law in Its
Political Settings,* ed. L. Foxhall & A. D. E. Lewis, Oxford 1996, pp. 57-72.

The scholar, for whom the oaths constitute the most important and crucial element in a
settlement of the disputes, is G. Thür, who claims that the early legal, or pre-legal, procedures were based on taking the oaths from both litigants. Then it was the role of a judge to
decide which party was right. His deeply interesting analysis consists in comparing the
Homeric society with the Gortyn code. The very few mentions referring to the legal procedures in Homer do not permit to accept this interpretation as the fully proved statement.
Nevertheless it is still one of the most instructing theories.

[75] V. E h r e n b e r g, *op.cit.,* pp. 10-11.

[76] *Ibidem,* Ehrenberg sees in θέμις the norm and sort of unwritten code of aristocracy,

That does not necessarily refer to the noblemen, but we cannot forget that in the first Homeric epic we, as a matter of fact, deal exclusively with aristocracy. Almost every custom, norm or order ruling the noble can be in due course transferred to the whole society. As an example we can quote the custom, or rather the rule, that tells a host to provide his guest with all that is due to strangers, ἅ τε ξείνοις θέμις ἐστιν.[77] It is also θέμις for the councillors to sit by the king and give counsels: (Il. 24, 650-653)

ἐκτὸς μὲν δὴ λέξο γέρον φίλε, μή τις 'Αχαιῶν
ἐνθάδ' ἐπέλθησιν βουληφόρος, οἵ τέ μοι αἰεὶ
βουλὰς βουλεύουσι παρήμενοι, ἢ θέμις ἐστί;

What attracts our attention in these words spoken by Achilles to Priam is the tone of Achilles' voice showing mockery, ἐπικερτομέων. The irony of the Greek hero does not, however, harm the meaning of θέμις. He addresses Priam mockingly using the phrase that would be quite appropriate in other circumstances.

Achilles means also more or less the same when he refuses to bathe until the body of his beloved friend is put on fire and buried. (Il. 23. 44): οὐ θέμις ἐστὶ λοετρὰ καρήατος ἆσσον ἱκέσθαι.

The grief and sorrow possessing Achilles forbid him to take care of his appearance. It seems to him unthinkable as long as the body of Patroclus still waits for burial. In that line it becomes quite clear that θέμις does not signify "a rule" or "a custom"; even "a norm" would be too strong; here this is a personal feeling that tells a man not to do something; it is the man himself who judges, what should be done and that is in our opinion, the only difference between this passage and the other, where the expression: "οὐ θέμις ἐστι" was already found.[78] By the death of Patroclus it was only the god, who did not let the helmet fall down to the ground, before it was ordered. In the case of Poseidon on the battlefield, with whom οὐ θέμις ἐστι for men to fight, the knights felt and recognized what was not permitted, but the denial came from above.

---

and in opposition to G. G l o t z (op.cit., p. 21) he does not refer it only to noblemen, but emphacizes its power as a convention within the society as a whole.

[77] Il. 11.777-779: ταφὼν δ' ἀνόρουσεν 'Αχιλλεύς,
ἐς δ' ἄγε χειρὸς ἑλών, κατὰ δ' ἑδριάασθαι ἄνωγε,
ξείνιά τ' εὖ παρέθηκεν, ἅ τε ξείνοις θέμις ἐστίν.
αὐτὰρ ἐπεὶ τάρπημεν ἐδητύος ἠδὲ ποτῆτος,
A. T. M u r r a y's translation (op.cit. I, p. 539): and Achilles seizes woth wonder, snang up, and took us by the hand and led us in, and bade us to be seated, and he set before us abundant entertaiment, all that is the due of strangers.

[78] Il. 14. 386, 16. 798.

Certainly, if any rules, customs or, at least advised ways of behaviour, exist there are also people, who do not respect them, either not knowing them (the case of Cyklopes in the "Odyssey") or simply not obeying them.

The "Iliad" mentions two such examples; the first one proves that θέμις can refer to a god as well as to a mortal man. The one, who does not know θέμις, is Ares (Il. 5. 761):

ἄφρων, ὃς οὔ τινα οἶδε θέμιστα. Hera, who complains to Zeus about Ares, calls him "madan, who regardth not any law".[79] Ares has no φρήν, he cannot recognize what can, and what cannot be done; in that sense he is the prototype of the Cyklops. His behaviour is caused by pure instinct, he let himself do anything to satisfy his temper, and his actions are frantic and almost crazy. Inferring from this picture, we may guess, what θέμις implays; one, who knows θέμις, knows what is permitted. He knows it because he feels it. The basis is altogether the same: ability to restrain one's emotional wishes and to subject them to the θέμις. It may be argued (together with V. Ehrenberg), that what we get here is the trace of social connection. In order to be a part of a group one should recognize the same rules. On this stage of the social development these rules are still to great extend a matter of intuition, as they are not codified. Nevertheless, they do exist and make life possible. θέμις even in the "Iliad" becomes a very important part of the set of this rules. It is hardly an easy task to provide its clear and uncomplicated definition, but there cannot be any doubt that this term plays certain role in the consolidation of the society.

The next passage, Il. 9.63, emphasizes that statement even stronger:

ἀφρήτωρ ἀθέμιστος ἀνέστιός ἐστιν ἐκεῖνος
ὃς πολέμου ἔραται ἐπιδημίου ὀκρυόεντος.

A clanless, lawless, heartless man is he who loveth dread strife among his own folk.[80]

The accumulation of adjectives is natural rhetoric[81] and it has been put on purpose.

Ἀφρήτωρ is derived from φρήτρη and means "without bratherhood, with no social bounds"[82], that is an outsider, someone standing beside the society.

---

[79] transl. A. T. M u r r a y, *op.cit.* I, p. 251.

[80] *Ibidem,* I, p. 387.

[81] B. H a i n s w o r t h, *The Iliad: A Commentary,* vol. III, pp. 67-68.

[82] see: Liddel-Scott, the Greek - English Lexicon, B. Hainsworth (*op.cit.*, p. 67) marks, that the notion of a phratry does not refer to the Homeric society, but comes from the time of the author (quotation according to A. A n d r e w s, *Hermes* 89 (1961), p. 12.

'Aνέστιος - without hearth and home, homeless and 'Aθέμιστοςὰ - knowing no law or, what seems to be more correct translation: not knowing or recognizing what is right, what suits its own society. The combination of these three adjectives is hardly a matter of coincidence. these two line of the text describe an an-social element: one, who is able to put the whole society in danger by inferring an inner strife.

There is still one more way in which θέμις is used in the "Iliad". It designates an order, almost the natural law, that makes things happen like they do. In that context θέμις appears in the book 9th, 134 and 276. Agamemnon, while trying to reconcile Achilles by giving him back his beloved Breseis, makes an oath, that he never "went up into her bad never had dalliance with her as is the appointed way of mankind, even of men and women"[83] – ἤ θέμις ἀνθρώπων τέλει, ἀνδρῶν ἤ δὲ γυναικῶν.

Further in the "Odyssey" this meaning will be broadened to the sphere of the whole family's life referring to the relationships between a wife and a husband and between a child and a parent as well. Here, as there is no legal marriage mentioned, it concerns rather natural behaviour, which sticks to the certain and generally accepted norm.

Complex meaning of the θέμις in the "Iliad" cannot be restricted to one main sense. This term plays too important role in the image of social relations binding the members of the community described by Homer. The next work, the "Odyssey", stresses different aspects of the notion and shows the development of θέμις which, in the later Homeric epic, becomes the most important term describing the order among men.

---

[83] transl. A. T. M u r r a y, op.cit., I, p. 393.

Θέμις in the "Odyssey".

In the later Homeric epic the meaning of θέμις is comparable to this of the "Iliad". It is also complex and significant. In most works referring to the subject both epics are discussed together[1], which inevitably implies that the sense of the term is the same. To a certain extent this opinion is correct, nevertheless it can be argued that in the "Odyssey" θέμις (like other terms) had already achieved a little higher niveau. Its development had been in progress and the results can be seen. It may seem a little bit surprising that, while there is general consent regarding major differences between the two Homeric masterpieces in many respects, this peculiar aspect is almost always omitted.

Let us consider in the first place the name of the goddess Θέμις (Themis). In the "Odyssey" one comes across it only once, Od. 2. 68 -69.[2] This passage was already discussed, but it is still worth recalling that Themis does not appear as a person, as it used to be in the "Iliad". Her function has been broadened and now it seems quite natural that Telemachus calls her name during his first public appearance. He calls Themis "who loses and gathers the assemblies of men".[3] This long predicate suggests that the goddess has been associated with this function for a long time. Furthermore, it is she who turns out to be more important at this moment; the name of Zeus is described only by a common adjective: "Olympian", whereas her name is given a specific account of her role. Certainly, the name of the highest Olympian ruler strengthens the authority of a minor deity.[4] Like other Olympians Themis in the "Odyssey" has changed her personal character; she is no longer Θέμις καλλιπάρηος, "of the fair cheeks"; she is a serious goddess who rules a certain region of human community's life.

---

[1] For example: R. Hirzel, E. Wolf, K.Latte; V. Ehrenberg belongs to the few who emphacizes the differences.

[2] Od. 2. 68-69: λίσσομαι ἠμὲν Ζηνὸς 'Ολυμπίου ἠδὲ Θέμιστος,

ἥ τ' ἀνδρῶν ἀγορὰς ἠμὲν λύει ἠδὲ καθίζει

[3] transl. A. T. M u r r a y, *The Odyssey*, LOEB, vol. I, London 1995, p. 51.

[4] *A Commenntary on Homer's Odyssey*, ed. A. H e u b e c k, S. W e s t, J. B. H a i n s w o r t h, Oxford 1988, vol. I, p. 135;

The close association with Zeus will become a common ideal later, since Hesiod; here θέμις signifies "traditional order of things, whether it depends merely on human convention".

The change the meaning of θέμις and its increasing role in governing the life of a community, especially that of noblemen, has been already claimed by V. Ehrenberg, who examined this process in the "Iliad".[5] According to his analysis, it has been proved that θέμις developed from the term denoting the rulers will (based on divine authority) into the main point of reference, the basic rule of the noble society. This thesis, being generally true, can be fully applied only to the "Odyssey". In the "Iliad", θέμις is barely associated with the royal power.

The meaning closely related to this sense of θέμις occurs only once in the book 16[th][6], where the wooers are planning an attempt on Telemachus' life and are trying to secure the help of Amphinomus. He, being the most decent of the impudent noblemen, tends to avoid such a situation and makes his answer safely dependable on the divine will, Od. 16. 400-405:

ὦ φίλοι, οὐκ ἂν ἐγώ γε κατακτείνειν ἐθέλοιμι
Τηλέμαχον; δεινὸν δὲ γένος βασιλήϊόν ἐστι
κτείνειν; ἀλλὰ πρῶτα θεῶν εἰρώμεθα βουλάς.
εἰ μέν κ' αἰνήσωσι Διὸς μεγάλοιο θέμιστες,
αὐτός τε κτενέω τούς τ' ἄλλους πάντας ἀνώξω;
εἰ δέ κ' ἀποτρωπῶσι θεοί, παύσασθαι ἄνωγα."

Friends, I surely would not choose to kill Telemachus; a dread thing is to slay one of royal stock. Nay, let us first seek to learn the will of the gods. If the oracles of great Zeus approve, I will myself slay him, and bid all the others do so; But, if the gods turn us from the act, I bid you desist.[7]

Perhaps the moral attitude of Amphinomus, who can be deterred from a murder only by the fright of gods or of a king, leaves much to be desired, still it is better than that of his comrades. In his speech at least two aspects deserve to be pointed out: δεῖνον γένος βασιλήϊον κτείνειν suggests that some authority possessed by kings in the "Iliad" was preserved, although no further explanation referring to that statement is included. There is no mention of divine support and favour offered to the "basileis, who hold a sceptre". However, it may be assumed that Amphinomus means just the complications connected with killing of someone coming from a mighty family, whose revenge can turn out to be dangerous. Special protection of Zeus

---

[5] V. E h r e n b e r g, *Die Rechtsidee in frühen Griechentum,* Leipzig 1921, pp. 12-13.

[6] See A. H o e k s t r a, *A Commentary on Homer's Odyssey,* Vol. II, Oxford 1988, p. 196, p. 283; θέμιστες can be associated with Zeus and royal power. Maybe in Mycenae (cf. Webster) this was a term for "due". Further, it tends to denote "custom" and can be used as a synonym of δίκη.

[7] Transl. A. T. M u r r a y, *op. cit.,* vol. II, p. 145.

must be rejected, as the next lines make it clear that he can accept the murder of a king's son. At least there is an opportunity of divine approval; otherwise there would be no sense in seeking the oracle. Had the authority of a king been supported by Zeus' power, as it was in the "Iliad", there would have been no sense in asking the supreme god about his opinion regarding the plot. Zeus, to whom kings used to be especially close in the "Iliad", may be against them.[8]

The next thing that attracts our attention is the bare fact of asking about Διὸς μεγάλοιο θέμιστας. They are no longer the divine dooms, ordinances. The will of gods may be asked and accepted; that is what the wooers eventually did.[9] But it is something new, that a mortal man can take initiative and does not have to wait till the deity tells him what to do.

Θέμιστες begin to denote divine answers for human questions given not directly, but by signs and oracles. Θέμιστες are again closely connected with βουλαί, gods' will. The meaning of the word βουλή comprises both: decision and the advice (councel), and both the senses can be found in the term "oracle".[10] This may imply that being oracles the βουλαί and θέμιστες of Zeus can be put into practice by pious men, but at the same time rejected or omitted by the others.

The only situation when a king is said to θεμιστεύειν refers to Odysseus' trip to the Underworld. The hero claims to have seen in Hades the former king of Crete, Minos.[11] That passage was already mentioned in the chapter about δίκη, and it has already been pointed out that any comparisons to the Christian image of final judgement should be avoided. The hero saw Minos

---

[8] V. E h r e n b e r g, op.cit., p. 14.

[9] Od., 20. 240-247: ὡς οἱ μὲν τοιαῦτα πρὸς ἀλλήλους ἀγόρευον;
μνηστῆρες δ' ἄρα Τηλεμάχῳ θάνατόν τε μόρον τε
ἤρτυον; αὐτὰρ ὁ τοῖσιν ἀριστερὸς ἤλυθεν ὄρνις,
αἰετὸς ὑψιπέτης, ἔχε δὲ τρήρωνα πέλειαν.
τοῖσιν δ' ἀΑμφίνομος ἀγορήσατο καὶ μετέειπεν;
"ὦ φίλοι, οὐχ ἥμιν συνθεύσεται ἤδε γε βουλή,
Τηλεμάχοιο φόνος; ἀλλὰ μνησώμεθα δαιτός."
ὣς ἔφατ' Ἀμφίνομος, τοῖσιν δὴ ἐπιήνδανε μῦθος.

[10] R. H i r z e l (Themis, Dike, und Verwandtes, Hildesheim 1966, pp. 20-21) emphasises this aspect of θέμιστες, which agrees with the rest of his analysis of that notion.

[11] Od. 11. 568-570: ἔνθ' ἦ τοι Μίνωα ἴδον, Διὸς ἀγλαὸν υἱόν,
χρύσεον σκῆπτρον ἔχοντα θεμιστεύοντα νέκυσσιν,
ἥμενον; οἱ δέ μιν ἀμφὶ δίκας εἴροντο ἄνακτα,
ἥμενοι ἐσταότες τε, κατ' εὐρυπυλὲς Ἄϊδος δῶ.

The Hades of king Minos is absolutely different from the rest of the Underworld; ghosts here are able to think and reason - see: D. P a g e, The Homeric Odyssey, Oxford 1955, p. 24.

θεμιτεύοντα νέκυσσιν, golden sceptre in his hand, surrounded by the dead asking for δίκας. The function that Minos performs in the Underworld, is simply the continuation of his activity in life.[12] He, the ruler, ἄναξ, holds the sceptre as the attribute of his authority "giving judgements"[13], "hielt bei den Toten Gericht mit dem goldenen Szepter"[14] The translation seems to be quite clear, nevertheless there are some difficulties, when one tries to imagine, what exactly Minos is doing. For M. Gagarin[15] this passage illustrates briefly the legal process in preliterate Greece. There is a judge and the opponents who brought their cases in front of him voluntarily (in this scene it is just an assumption), and the whole thing takes place in public. As it has already been reported, that interpretation has not been unanimously accepted.[16] Let us for the moment follow this interpretation, which will enable us to formulate questions concerning this particular scene. According to M. Gagarin, the scene of judgement, though different in a few aspects from the famous scene depicted on Achilles' shield, illustrates the procedure similar to that described in the 18th book of the "Iliad" (Il. 18. 497-508). Instead of judges there is only one judge, so the litigants have no choice. On the other hand, they bring their disputes in front of king Minos voluntarily. As regards the nature of these disputes, as well as of the settlements, there is no mention of it. Gagarin's claim that the cases of homicide are probably not included cannot be verified.

The most important question that comes to one's mind is: what sort of authority is possessed by Minos? Does he give judgements in the strict sense, that is: does he decide which party is right and which is wrong? Is there any relation of his θεμιστεύειν to the same verb used in Cyklops' characteristic?

---

[12] A. H e u b e c k, *A Commentary on Homer's Odyssey, op.cit.*, p. 111.

[13] Transl. A. T. M u r r a y, *op.cit.*, vol. I, pp. 426-427.

[14] Transl. A. W e i h e r, *Homer, Odysssee und Homerischen Hymnen,* München 1990, p. 233:

Da aber sah ich Minos, den herrlichen Sohn der Zeus; er
Saß und hielt bei den Toten Gericht mit dem goldenen Szepter.
Und ihn herum aber fragten die Toten dem herrn nach dem Urteil,
Saßenund standen dabei vor den breiten Toren zum Hades.

[15] M. G a g a r i n, *Early Greek Law,* Berkeley-Los Angeles-London 1986, p. 33.

[16] The fervent discussion referring to the legal procedure and the role of an oath in early Greek society was reported in the previous chapter. The most important opponent to Gagarin's theory is G. Thür, who treats this hypothesis with a great deal of distrust; in his opinion it is purely speculative and has no basis in other texts, that can be instructive in the subject, mainly the preserved codices of Greek law; see: G. T h ü r, *Oaths and Dispute Settlement in Ancient Greek Law,* in: *Greek Law in Its Political Settings,* ed. L. Foxhall & A. D. E. Lewis, Oxford 1996, pp. 57-72.

The first question can be answered with nothing more than a hypothesis: Minos, being a king, delivers his decisions and, like in scenes of the Underworld, it is possible that also that one resembles the custom of the "Ilaid", which in the "Odyssey" plays no further role? In the "Odyssey", Minos preserved the authority of a king, which belonged to the kingship, as described in the earlier epic. The second suggestion must be analysed with caution. Minos' power is high above the niveau of savage Cyclopes, nevertheless they have something in common. The main difference consists in the fact that θεμιστεύειν of Minos concerns the subjects who accept that power and do it voluntarily; it is a public procedure and does not refer to a family. On the other hand, it can be assumed that the decisions of Minos are ultimate and, perhaps, there is no retreat from them.

The most impressive passage referring to this phase of the term's development is the great part of book 9, the adventure of Cyclopes.

It has been proved that the story of Polyphemus belongs to the much more numerous set of adventures recounted in the whole Europe.[17] As D. Page proved[18], the same pattern is repeated several times and there is no reason to believe that at least part of these stories had been based on Homeric epics. On the contrary, some parts of the "Odyssey" belong to the universal folk-tales and, as a matter of fact, have nothing to do with the main theme. Furthermore, there are certain inconsistencies in the Homeric version of this particular adventure.[19] What is worth pointing out is the way how Homer repeated the popular story changing some details in order to adopt it to his own purposes. The general pattern, as claimed by D. Page, goes as follows: the Hero (the myth of Returning Hero) is kept prisoner by a giant shepherd, who eats Hero's comrades. The Hero, thanks to his cunning and brilliant mind, blinds the monster and escapes in the disguise of a sheep or attached under the sheep's belly. All the elements create a well-constructed unity. The giant sets fire to cook people, so there is fire and burning stick or a spit. Then he devours a few people, and having eaten the enormous meal he falls asleep, so the Hero can act. The monster is a shepherd and sleeps together with his cattle, so he must let them out in the

---

[17] All these stories were collected and published in 1904 by Oskaar Hackmann; see: D. P a g e, *The Homeric Odyssey*, Oxford 1955, p. 3.

[18] D. P a g e, *op. cit.*, pp. 3-5.

[19] *Ibidem*: Odysseus visited the island of Aiolus at the Far West and suddenly was taken to the Far East to entertain the serious of adventures resembling these of the Argonauts or being partly connected with this myth (Circe - Aietes' sister, Wondering Rocks, the wrath of Helios, Sirens).

morning opening the way for the Hero to escape. The fact that he has got only one eye makes the Hero's action simpler and easier.

The story told by Homer differs in a few respects from the popular version. The most important difference is the trick with the name of Nobody. As a matter of fact, this trick appears in another tale, the one about the struggle between a man and a demon, where the man tells his enemy that his name is Myself.[20]

As it has already been claimed, Polyphemus and his kin stand in opposition to the civilized community. Apart from δίκη, θέμις is used by the poet as one of the two main terms to draw a border line, in the strongest way marking the difference between civilized men and savage monsters. It is difficult to overestimate the meaning of the scenes in Polyphemus' cave. They describe not only one of the most dramatic and thrilling adventures of Odysseus, but, furthermore, provide the most basic criteria for defining an enlightened society, or just a society. What we have in the 9th book of the "Odyssey" is not the collision of two different political and social orders (cultures), which implies disappointment of the expectations of one side; there can be no collision, as there is only one culture represented by Odysseus and his company, who face a pre-social individual. The Cyclopes are described as:

Od. 9. 106: ἀθέμιστοι
Od. 9. 112-115: οὔτ' ἀγοραὶ βουληφόροι οὔτε θέμιστες,
ἀλλ' οἵ γ' ὑψηλῶν ὀρέων ναίουσι κάρηνα
ἐν σπέεσι γλαφυροῖσι, θεμιστεύει δὲ ἕκαστος
παίδων ἠδ' ἀλόχων, οὐδ' ἀλλήλων ἀλέγουσι.

Neither assemblies for council have they, nor appointed laws, but they dwell ion the peaks of lofty mountains in hollow caves, and each one is lawgiver to his children and his wives, and they have no regard for one another.[21]

Sie haben keine rechtliche Ordnung, beraten auch nicht in offner Versammlung(...) und jeder einzelne schaltet dortr über weiber und Kinder.[22]

---

[20] For further analysis see: D. P a g e, op.cit., pp. 5-7.

[21] Transl. A. T. M u r r a y, op.cit. vol. I, p. 311.

[22] *Sie haben auch keine*
Rechtliche Ordnung, beraten auch nicht in offner Versammlung,
Darum hausen się auch auf den Gipfeln des hohen Gebirges
Nur in geräumigen Grotten, und jeder einzelne schaltet
Dort über Weiber und Kinder, und keine sorgt für den anderen. Transl. A. Weiher, Hom-

To this fragment one should add the passage already quoted (Od. 9.215), where it is said that Polyphemus does not know δίκας οὔτε θέμιστας. Translating this words as "justice" and "law", A. T. Murray cautiously adds that in the Greek text both words are plural, what indicates not abstract, but concrete meaning; law is a body of traditional decrees or dooms.[23]

Ohne Kunde von Recht und Gesetz - the German translation brings an abstract interpretation.[24]

Cyclops live alone, they do not need one another, so every household is self-sufficient. That alone would not make them savage, as it can be referred to Greek οἶκοι as well. The point is that they do not build any sort of community, they do not meet at public gatherings to discuss public matters, they do not need any βουλαί. As they do not take any decisions, they do not know any θέμιστας, they do not know any ἀγορά. No element, so important in the Achaean society, exist here: neither meeting, nor public discussion, nor taking decisions regarding common matters. In this context, θέμιστες do not signify the divine or royal will, although some scholars translate the negative adjective ἀθέμιστοι as not having θέμιστες, that is "divinely appointed ordinances".[25] Ἀθέμιστος means "lawless", where "law" designates a commonly approved rule, based on a commonly taken decision. The meaningful association of θέμις, ἀγορά and βουλή has already been pointed out, but now it becomes even more clear thanks to the negation. There is no direct mention of the divine cult, but it may be assumed, that nothing of that sort exists in Cyclops' world. Indeed, Polyphemus himself makes it quite clear that he and his fellows do not worship any divine power except for themselves.[26] They do not recognise the divine power of the Olympian gods, nor do they fear divine wrath. The only factor governing their deeds is their own θυμός.

For V. Ehrenberg the Cyclops do miss the gathering (Versammlung), rules (δίκαι, Rechte) and the divine orders (die Gebote der Götter) - θέμιστες, which, taken together, constitute the basis of a political society.[27] The only

---

ers *Odyssee und Homerische Hymnen,* München 1990, p. 181.

[23] A. T. M u r r a y, *op.cit.,* vol. I, p. 317.

[24] see: A. W e i h e r, *op.cit.,* p. 184.

[25] A. H e u b e c k, *A Commentary on Homer's Odyssey, op.cit.,* p. 21, to compare with A. T. Murray's "lawless folk", *op.cit.* vol. I, p. 311, and A. Weiher's "dei gesetzlos leben", *op.cit.,* p. 181.

[26] Od. 9. 275-278: οὐ γὰρ Κύκλωπες Διὸς αἰγιόχου ἀλέγουσιν
οὐδὲ θεῶν μακάρων, ἐπεὶ ἦ πολὺ φέρτεροί εἰμεν;
οὐδ' ἂν ἐγὼ Διὸς ἔχθος ἀλευάμενος πεφιδοίμην
οὔτε σεῦ οὔθ' ἑτάρων, εἰ μὴ θυμός με κελεύοι.

[27] V. E h r e n b e r g, *op.cit.,* p. 14.

doubt that can be caused by this statement is connected with the meaning of θέμιστες. Do they really denote ordinances of the gods?

It is obvious that the divine cult lies in the beginning of the social order[28] and it is one of the elements missing on the Cyclopes' island. Polyphemus' contempt for divine dooms is emphasized *expressis verbis* in the lines mentioned above (Od. 9. 275-278) and expressed by his treatment of strangers. Moreover, in the following analysis V. Ehrenberg himself in stresses the "social" aspect of θέμις, proving, that it contains the notion of the will to belong to a community (Willen zur Gemeinshaft).[29] Certainly it constitutes the most important aspect of θέμις in the whole passage. It also clarifies the meaning of ἀθέμιστος - someone, who does not belong and does not want to be a part of a community, who does not care for any common rules and does not need them to make his own life better or possible at all. The group of such individuals resembles a set of elements having no connection with one another. Loss of one element cannot destroy the whole structure, because there is no structure, no coherent unity. Perhaps a danger is the only moment when Cyclopes show a trace of social bond: they react to Polyphemus' cries and gather to check, what the matter is.[30] Their interest, however, can be explained by both curiosity and disturbance (they were woken at night).

In this situation it may seem rather surprising that the poet used the word θεμιστεύειν in order to characterize Cyclopes' family lives. Every Cyclops is said to θεμιστεύειν παίδων ἠδ' ἀλόχων (Od. 9. 114-115) - "be a lawgiver to his children and wives" (A.T. Murray), "schaltet über Weiber und Kinder (A. Weiher) - more or less "to rule his wives[31] and children". He decides about the life of his family members and, most probably, his authority is the only one known in his οἶκος. It may be comparable to the of a king from the "Iliad". R. Hirzel correctly calls it "ein patrirchalisches Regiment".[32]

---

[28] Although the connection between religion and the beginning of the society can be discussed, see: U. W e s e l, *Geschichte des Rechtsvon Frühformen bis zum Vertrag von Maastricht,* München 1997, M. G a g a r i n, *op.cit.,* pp. 34 ff.

[29] V. E h r e n b e r g, *op.it.,* p. 15.

[30] Od. 9. 398-406.

[31] Ἄλοχος does not necessarily define a spouse, it may as well be just "someone's partner in bed"; besides the poet uses plural form, that implies either polygamy, or, what is more probable, cohabitation without any specific form of legal relationship. For example, Homer uses this word in Od. 3.403 and in Il. 1. 114, where Klitaimnestra is called κουρίδιη ἄλοχος, the wedded wife. Maybe the adjective κουρίδιη is added to make the form of this relationship quite clear.

[32] R. H i r z e l, *op.cit.,* p. 27.

Cyclopes seem to dwell on the patriarchal stage of development.[33]

However, the analysis presented by R. Hirzel turns out to be concentrated on the notion of the Rath, the advice, to too great an extent.[34] There can be no certainty as to the limits of a Cyclops' power over his household; we are not told in the details whether it concerns the life and death of the subjects, but it is reasonable to assume that there are no limits, since the only decisive (counting) factor is the will and "heart", θυμός, of the Cyclops.

According to R. Hirzel[35] the translation of θεμιστεύειν as "giving laws or orders" should be out of question, but it is still recognized as an announcement of a master's will, coming from some source beyond the reach of the subjects.

There is no trace of a counsel, or of seeking advice. The picture is clear: the master of a house decides about everything. The discussion is barely permitted and his orders should, at most probability, be taken seriously and put into practice without being subjected to any analysis. His rule, θεμιστεύειν, has no divine background, it is merely the utterance of the free, unrestricted will, the will of the stronger. He is the only source of laws and rules in his small environment, and in this sense his authority can be compared to the role of a god in the world outside. Still, the verb θεμιστεύειν is to be treated quite seriously and there is no reason, except for the translator's intuition, to see intentional irony in the use of this word here.[36] Cyclops do not know any θέμιστες, because they do not obey any common rules or decisions, but perhaps there was no better word to describe their role in a family. There is also one more explanation: Cyclops do use θέμιστες in a family, although probably they are only the source of these orders, not the subjects of this power; being at this stage of development, as they are, they have still not discovered, that such solutions could be applied to a larger group of people, beyond the limits of a single family.[37]

The only phrase that can upset this distinct image is found in Od. 1. 70-71:

ἀντίθεον Πολύφημον, ὅου κράτος ἐστὶ μέγιστον

πᾶσιν Κυκλώπεσσι· - *the godlike Polyphemus, whose might is greatest among all the Cyclops.*[38]

---

[33] For a brief analysis of this term see: U. W e s e l, *op.cit.*

[34] R. H i r z e l, *op.cit.*, pp. 28-30.

[35] *Ibidem.*

[36] A. H e u b e c k, *A Commentary on Homer's Odysey,* vol. I, *op.cit.*, p. 84.

[37] Some scholars claim, that Homer just could not find the better word.

[38] Transl. A. T. M u r r a y.

D. Page claims that these lines describe Polyphemus as the king of all the Cyclopes.[39] This does not agree with the popular folk tale, where the giant is characterized as a lonely outsider. In Page's interpretation Polyphemus is the master and this is the reason why other giants come to rescue him so promptly. This statement, however in accord with the words, does not seem plausible. The authors of " A Commentary on Homer's *Odyssey*"[40] are much more correct. They emphasize the fact that the epithet ἀντίθεον should not be understood as characterising the power of the Cyclops as being the same as the might of Zeus, but, simply, marking the difference between Polyphemus, the son of Poseidon, and another personality bearing the same name (Il. 1. 264). The expression κράτος μέγιστον is applied to Zeus (Od.5.4, Il. 2.118, 9.25) as to the supreme ruler, but it can hardly refer to Polyphemus in the very same meaning. It should rather mean that Polyphemus is the strongest of all the Cyclopes. It is generally accepted that κράτος (κάρτος) in Homer refers especially to physical strength.[41] Furthermore, the single mention of κράτος μέγιστον cannot change the meaning of another, more complex, description of Polyphemus. Had he been a ruler, he would not have described other Cyclopes, as he did it, stressing their independence and freedom. The mention has however some meaning for the hero of the epic: the power of Odysseus' enemy should correspond to the talents of the king. The mightier the opponent, the more glamorous victory. Odysseus being a great hero himself deserves a fight with the great enemy.

The picture drawn in the 9th book of the "Odyssey" excludes any suggestion of Polyphemus being a king. This would imply, that Cyclopes are a community ruled by a master, and it is obvious that such an interpretation is out of question.

The ninth book of the "Odyssey" provides one more passage that can be very instructive at this point (Od. 9. 187-189):

ἔνθα δ' ἀνὴρ ἐνίαυε πελώριος, ὅς ῥα τὰ μῆλα
οἶος ποιμαίνεσκεν ἀπόπροθεν; οὐδὲ μετ' ἄλλους
πωλεῖτ', ἀλλ' ἀπάνευθεν ἐὼν ἀθεμίστια ᾔδη.

There a monstrous man was wont to sleep, who shepherded his flocks

---

[39] D. P a g e, *op.cit.*, p. 6.
[40] *A Commentary on Homer's Odyssey, op.cit.*, p. 6.
[41] see: *A Greek-English Lexicon*, ed. by Liddel and Scott, *op.cit.*, p. 991, Il.7.147, 13.484, Od. 9.393.

alone and afar, and mingled not with others, but lived with his heart set on lawlessness.[42]

It is once more emphasized that Polyphemus is not familiar with θέμιστες; on the contrary, he knows what is opposed to θέμις. The Commentary[43] points out, that all the expressions used to draw a picture of a giant illustrate the lack of humanity. He and his kin live in caves, perhaps because they do not know how to built houses, they do not know any τέχνη.

The expression, as a characteristic epithet describing the Cyclops, is repeated in 9. 248, where Poliphemus is called ἀθεμίστια εἰδώς again.

The whole tale about the monstrous son of Poseidon, apart from being the best constructed of all the stories included in the later Homeric epic[44], explains in a very distinct way the Homeric view on the definition of human community, a definition by negation. Almost in every respect the Cyclopes lack the basic qualities that create a society. They do not built houses, they do not know how to construct a ship[45], there are no craftsmen among them[46], they do not till the soil[47], they live apart from one another. Besides, what is most important, they do not have any gatherings, any public meetings, and they do not have any δίκας, any θέμιστας. The last evaluation is repeated most often, so it seems natural that it was the most significant and distinct term. Θέμις missing was equal to not having any social connection, i. e., a constructive factor binding the individuals and making a unity out of single elements.

The condemnatory adjective ἀθέμιστος is used only in few places more. It expresses poet's full resentment of Penelope's wooers and their reprehensible behaviour.

In the 17th book (17.178) Odysseus assisted by Athene carries out a final test over the wooers. Still in the disguise of a beggar he goes round the table, at which the young noblemen are seated, and asks for a bit of bread. The purpose is to find out which of the wooers are righteous (ἐναίσιμοι) and

---

[42] transl. A.T. M u r r a y, *op.cit.* vol. I, p. 315.

[43] *A Commentary on Homer's Odyssey,* vol. II, p. 25.

[44] D. P a g e, *op.cit.,* p. 9.

[45] Od. 9, 116-130.

[46] *Ibidem.*

[47] Od. 9. 105-108: ἐνθεν δὲ προτέρω πλέομεν ἀκαχήμενοι ἦτορ.
Κυκλώπων δ' ἐς γαῖαν ὑπερφιάλων ἀθεμίστων
ἰκόμεθ', οἵ ῥα θεοῖσι πεποιθότες ἀθανάτοισιν
οὔτε φυτεύουσιν χερσὶν φυτὸν οὔτ' ἀρόωσιν,
"There we sailed on, grived at heart, and we come to the land of the Cyclops, overweening and lawless folk, who, trusting in the immortal gods, plant nothing with their hands nor plough" - transl. A. T. Murray, *op.cit.* vol. I, p. 311.

which are lawless (ἀθέμιστοι).[48] The trial is, as a matter of fact, not necessary, since the goddess has already made up her mind to destroy all of them. Odysseus, however, is probably not aware of the divine decision. Besides, the additional humiliation of the hero provides further reasons for his revenge and makes it not only understandable, but, moreover, lawful and decent.[49] At least some wooers are not going to pass that exam, the most striking example being Cteisippus. This young and wealthy noble of Same is described by the very same expression as Polyphemus - ἀνὴρ ἀθεμίστια εἰδώς (Od. 20. 294) - "a man with his heart set on lawlessness".[50] He throws an ox hoof at the beggar, who happens to be the real master of the house. This is Athene who makes it happen in order to make the hero suffer even more and to make him firm in his plans to kill the wooers. Nevertheless, what Ctesippos has done, places him in the same niveau as the savage Cyclops. Neither they nor he recognized the law of hospitality. As J. Russo emphasizes it[51], his behaviour is a nasty mockery of the custom (θέμις) of hospitality and resembles "a horrible parody of the proper procedure for giving guests their due".[52]

The next passage, where ἀθεμίστιος appears, belongs to a slightly different class. Its importance can be inferred from the fact that it happens to be a part of Odysseus' speech, in which the hero expresses the basic moral theory. However, it is not a coherent and fully logically consistent set of sentences. In the 18th book of the "Odyssey" (18. 125-150) Odysseus tells the story describing his own, i. e., the beggar's, life. The beggar's happiness and his later misfortune are supposed to illustrate human condition and serve as an example for the others. The human fortune swings as a wheel and it can change for better or for worse without warning. In the first lines it is made clear that the deeds of a man have nothing to do with the course and direction of this change; in other words: the gods decide about human lot without any consideration for the quality of human actions. Whether they are good, or evil, makes no difference. Further the tone is

---

[48] Od. 17. 360-364: αὐτὰρ ᾽Αθήνη
ἄγχι παρισταμένη Λαερτιάδην ᾽Οδυσῆα
ὤτρυν᾽, ὡς ἂν πύρνα κατὰ μνηστῆρας ἀγείροι
γνοίη θ᾽ οἵ τινές εἰσιν ἐναίσιμοι οἵ τ᾽ ἀθέμιστοι;
ἀλλ᾽ οὐδ᾽ ὡς τιν᾽ ἔμελλ᾽ ἀπαλεξήσειν κακότητος.

[49] E. A. H a v e l o c k, *The Greek Concept of Justice,*Cambridge Mass. and London 1978.

[50] Transl. A.T. M u r r a y, *op.cit.* vol. II, p. 295.

[51] J. R u s s o, *A Commentry on Homer's Odyssey,* ed. J. Russo, M. Fernández-Galiano, A. Heubeck, Oxford 1992, vol. III, p. 121.

[52] *Ibidem.*

changed. As it has been emphasized by J. Russo[53], Odysseus, while describing his imagined misfortune, tends to show that the sudden change of his lot was, at least partly, connected with his bad deeds (ἀτάσθλ' ἔρεξα βίη καὶ κάρτεϊ εἴκων; Od. 18. 139). Such an approach makes it possible to give judgement on the wooers in the sentence, the general character of which should not be overlooked (Od. 18. 141-142):

τῶ μή τίς ποτε πάμπαν ἀνὴρ ἀθεμίστιος εἴη,
ἀλλ' ὅ γε σιγῆ δῶρα θεῶν ἔχοι, ὅττι διδοῖεν.

Therefore let no man ever be lawless at any time, but let him keep in silence whatever gifts the gods give.[54]

As J. Russo observed[55], the lack of logical consistency and the gap between the relativity of the verses 131-140 and the moral causality in the lines 141-142, should not trouble the modern reader. It is still reasonable to see in this passage "one of the first examples of early Greek speculative thought, striving to articulate a morally justifiable theodicy".[56] It is as well probable that Odysseus' intention is make Amphinomus leave, as it has already been suggested.[57]

Almost all other appearances of θέμις in the "Odyssey" are connected with the notion of what is fitting, what constitutes a custom. The range of the term is quite wide, since it refers to the life of a family being the norm ruling the relations between family members as well as to the relations to strangers. On that ground it became the social norm, introducing order into the society of noblemen and telling its members what they should do in particular circumstances. The examples are plenty at hand, the only doubt may concern the degree, to which the sense of θέμις is supported by the divine will. It is θέμις when a son greets his father (Od. 11. 450-451):

ἦ γὰρ τόν γε πατὴρ φίλος ὄψεται ἐλθών,
καὶ κεῖνος πατέρα προσπτύξεται, ἦ θέμις ἐστίν.

---

[53] *Ibidem.*
[54] transl. A. T. M u r r a y, *op.cit.*, vol. II, p. 211.
[55] J. R u s s o, *op.cit.*, p. 121.
[56] *Ibidem,* see also: W. N e s t l e, *op. cit.*, p. 23, or *Griechische Geistgeschichte,* Stuttgart 1941, where W. Nestle emphaticzes the importance of Od. 1. 32-34 interpreting these lines as the first trace of theodicy. In this passage Zeus says:
„ὦ πόποι, οἷον δή νυ θεοὺς βροτοὶ αἰτιόωνται.
ἐξ ἡμέων γάρ φασι κάκ' ἔμμεναι; οἱ δὲ καὶ αὐτοὶ
σφῆσιν ἀτασθαλίησιν ὑπὲρ μόρον ἄλγε' ἔχουσιν,
[57] J. R u s s o, *op.cit.*, pp. 80-81.

R. Hirzel translates θέμις in this passage as a custom[58], for V. Ehrenberg[59] this term belongs to social norms concerning the close family circle. The interpretation presented by R. Hirzel seems to be a little artificial; the behaviour of a son greeting his homecoming father can be explained not by the custom, but, usually, by the feelings: it should be so. This means: a child should greet his parent, therefore it is generally expected and becomes this, what is fitting, and what should be done, θέμις. The notion denotes "the traditional order of things, dependent either of human convention or nature", as it is defined by the authors of the commentary on the "Odyssey".[60]

The same concerns the reaction of a woman whose husband dies afar (Od. 14. 130):

ἢ θέμις ἐστὶ γυναικός, ἐπὴν πόσις ἄλλοθ' ὄληται.

R. Hirzel's translation "Gewohnheit", i. e., "habit", sounds odd.[61] A woman who had lost her husband tends to cry and nobody will ascribe it to the habit, although everybody expects such behaviour as being appropriate.

From the sphere of family life we may proceed now to social life, that is, to the rules of proper behaviour at table, the meet behaviour while as a stranger guest and as a host. We recognize that it is meet, or even right, as A. T. Murray translates the appropriate line[62], that Nestor answers Telemachus' request and tells him everything he knows about the heroes' returning home from Troy.[63] It has already been claimed that the king of Pylos is an example of a perfect ruler, a wise and well-brought man, respectable both for his authority and his wisdom; he is certainly the one who will always follow what is θέμις. His guests are equally well educated and at the beginning of the banquet they pour a libation in honour of the immortal gods (O. 3.45).[64] This particular θέμις may denote not only what is

---

[58] R. H i r z e l, op.cit., p. 40.

[59] V. E h r e n b e r g, op.cit., pp. 15-16.

[60] A Commentary on Homer's Odyssey, op.cit., vol. I, p. 135.

[61] R. H i r z e l, op.cit., p. 40.

[62] A. T. M u r r a y, op.cit., vol. I.

[63] Od. 3. 186-187: ὅσσα δ' ἐνὶ μεγάροισι καθήμενος ἡμετέροισι
πεύθομαι, ἢ θέμις ἐστί, δαήσεαι, οὐδέ σε κεύσω.

[64] Od. 3. 43- 48: εὔχεο νῦν, ὦ ξεῖνε, Ποσειδάωνι ἄνακτι;
τοῦ γὰρ καὶ δαίτης ἠντήσατε δεῦρο μολόντες.
αὐτὰρ ἐπὴν σπείσῃς τε καὶ εὔξεαι, ἢ θέμις ἐστί,
δὸς καὶ τούτῳ ἔπειτα δέπας μελιηδέος οἴνου
σπεῖσαι, ἐπεὶ καὶ τοῦτον ὀίομαι ἀθανάτοισιν
εὔχεσθαιρ πάντες δὲ θεῶν χατέουσ' ἄνθρωποι.

fitting, but also what is due to the gods. Association with the cult of a deity always strengthens the power of a term. Certainly, it can be argued that by that time the libation had already become a habitual part of a feast and was performed without a deeper thought given to it. However, this remark cannot be applied to Homeric epic, where divine presence in human life is not unusual. At the table in Nestor's palace there is also a goddess sitting. Though her presence is not discovered, pious people can always assume that sharing one's dinner with an immortal guest is not beyond the limits of reality.

Furthermore, since a common dining plays quite an important role in Homer, everything that rules this part of social life, must be regarded as significant. A feast, a banquet, seems to be the centre of human life. Homeric men, even mere slaves like Eumaeus, attach a great deal of attention to dining, especially in the presence of a stranger. A feast in Homer often accompanies important events in the life of a community. Homeric heroes do not talk about business without a precedent banquet.

A special place of a stranger guest and the law of hospitality have already been mentioned, but it seems worth emphasizing that not only δίκη or δίκαιον refer to this sphere of life. In the "Odyssey", it turns out to be particularly distinct in the passage in the 9th book (Od. 9. 266-268); Odysseus introduces himself to Polyphemus and explains for what purpose he and his fellows have come to the Cyclops' cave:

ἡμεῖς δ' αὖτε κιχανόμενοι τὰ σὰ γοῦνα
ἱκόμεθ', εἴ τι πόροις ξεινήϊον ἠὲ καὶ ἄλλως
δοίης δωτίνην, ἥ τε ξείνων θέμις ἐστίν.

On our part, thus visiting thee, have come as suppliants to thy knees, in the hope that thou wilt give us entertainment, or in other wise make some present, as is the due of strangers.[65]

Odysseus' mention of θέμις ξείνων sounds striking when faced with Polyphemus' horrible behaviour. As it has already been said, the Cyclops is an anti-social creature, and one of his characteristic features is that he does not recognize the law of hospitality.

On the opposite side we see Eumaeus, whose attitude towards the accepted rules and orders resembles that of Nestor. His action corresponds with his words (Od. 14. 56-58):

ξεῖν', οὔ μοι θέμις ἔστ', οὐδ' εἰ κακίων σέθεν ἔλθοι,

---

[65] Transl. A. T. M u r r a y, *op. cit.*, vol. I, p. 321.

ξεῖνον ἀτιμῆσαι; πρὸς γὰρ Διός εἰσιν ἅπαντες
ξεῖνοί τε πτωχοί τε

*Nay, stranger, it were not right of me, even though one meaner than you
were to come, to slight a stranger; for from Zeus are all strangers and
beggars.*[66]

The most elaborate, profound and decisive translation of these lines was
provided by R. Hirzel[67]: *Es steht mir nicht zu nach den göttlichen geordne-
ten und feststehenden Sittlichkeisgesetzen, deren Buch auch göttliche Be-
strafung zu fürchten hatte, Gastfreunde, Bettler zu missachten.*

This interpretation makes it clear that the law of hospitality has already
reached the level of a moral rule, but it seems to be rather difficult to prove.
W. Nestle claims that in Homer there is still no clear-cut division between
the custom (Sitte) and morals (Sittlichkeit).[68] On the other hand, it must be
said that in the case of Eumaeus it is even more difficult not to think about
morals. Moreover, as the reason of his conduct he gave not the opinion of
other people, but the divine order. Certainly, one could cut this discussion
by claiming that Eumaeus is just a good man and such people happen to
exist at every stage of the history of mankind.

The guest of Eumaeus, the beggar who appears to be Odysseus himself,
also proves that the savoir-vivre is known to him. When Eumaeus and
Telemachus discuss what they should do with their guest, he takes part in
the dispute, only after having politely explained that he interfered, because
it was meet, θέμις (Od. 16. 91): ὦ φίλ᾽, ἐπεί θήν μοι καὶ ἀμείψασθαι θέμις
ἐστίν, In that particular sentence it would be better to translate θέμις as "to
be permitted". The beggar's position and the subject of conversation makes
it apparent that this is the best way.

Although it may be surprising to compare the magnificent palace of
mighty Nestor to the poor shed of a swineherd, both scenes provide us with
an almost perfect model of social duties performed by a host and by his
guests. In both scenes the host is unaware of the fact that his behaviour is
going to bring him considerable profit. Both hosts, Nestor as well as
Eumaeus, do their best to entertain the strangers and neither of them is
aware of the true identity of these men. Nestor does not recognize Athene,
whose grace will be beneficial to Neleus' son, Eumaeus does not know that
he is just helping his master, which in due time will be appreciated by grate-

---

[66] *Ibidem,* vol. II, p. 41.
[67] R. H i r z e l, *op.cit.,* p. 28.
[68] W. N e s t l e, *op.cit.,* p. 39.

ful Odysseus. This picture could verify V. Ehrenberg's statement, according to which θέμις as a social norm refers exclusively to the community of noblemen.[69] Here a slave follows θέμις in the very same manner as a powerful king. Hence, we might infer that θέμις was a generally accepted norm, ruling not only the lives of rich and powerful knights, but also those of their humble subjects.

On the other hand, Eumaeus is by no means a mere slave; he had been taken prisoner as a youngster, but he comes from a royal family.[70] Describing him, Homer uses the same epithets as while describing his masters. That would imply that the scene in the shed of Eumaeus is a reflection of aristocratic life. The swineherd knows the rules, because he had the same background and he probably acquired a lot in the period of his slavery. His position in the οἶκος of Odysseus is higher than that of other servants and, at all probability, he can afford better maintenance than the others.[71] This seems reasonable, though one remark should be made: in Homer there is almost no other society, but aristocratic one. All the customs and norms described in the epics refer to the gentry, but it does not necessarily mean, that some of them cannot be applied to the people of a lower social status.

In the "Odyssey", we are shown for the first time, that a slave can be more decent than a nobleman and is also able to manifest it.[72]

The attitude towards simple people is dramatically changed as compared to the "Iliad", where the only representative of the people was generally despised, physically deterring, ugly Thersites.[73] Here, in the second epic, the world of noblemen is also inhabited by slaves and servants, its social structure is more complex and complete. The poet is even inclined to admit that people of lower condition possess some individual features, and that the adjectives describing behaviour as decent or indecent can also be referred to these sort of humans.

Everybody who wants to check whether the terms valid in the aristocratic circle are also employed among the people has to agree that it is

---

[69] V. E h r e n b e r g, *op.cit.*, pp. 16-17.

[70] Eumaeus is the son of Ctesios, the king of Syria island; he was kidnapped by the Phenicians and bought from them by Laertes - Od. 15. 403-484.

[71] For example: he can buy a slave himself, having paid for him with his own resources, notifying neither the lady of the house nor his old master. He must have had some money and a considerable authority. - Od. 14.449-452.

[72] Od. 17. 381: Ἀντίνο᾽, οὐ καλὰ καὶ ἐσθλὸς ἐὼν ἀγορεύεις.

[73] The briliant study conducted by K. Korus provides a different view on this personge presenting Thersits as the element of caricature of the a nobelman; see: *Die griechische Satire. Die theoretischen Grundlagen unnd ihre Anwendung auf Homers Epik*, Kraków 1991.

impossible to prove any of the two hypotheses given above. The aristocratic θέμις could have been adopted by lower social classes in a very natural way of copying the pattern. This would imply that elsewhere, outside the aristocratic world, θέμις would not be recognized; if there are no noblemen, there is no pattern.

In Homer, however, there is no other world, and we read either about aristocrats or people whose lives are closely connected with the life of the upper class. It must be reminded, that the society depicted by Homer cannot be regarded as a fully realistic image. Nevertheless, it reflects the major characteristics of a really existing community.

If this interpretation is accepted, the consequence is that θέμις ruled the life of the whole community, although the source of this term is to be found in the world of aristocracy. This suggests that V. Ehrenberg is right when he explains the etymology of noble names containing the suffix -θεμις by their connection with the word θέμις denoting a norm, not the deity.[74]

The "Odyssey" provides two more passages containing θέμις: Od.22. 286 as well as another passage, Od. 10. 73 refers to the law of hospitality; the latter turns out to be much more interesting.

In the 10th book, the hero recounts his second visit at the island of Aeolus. Odysseus arrived, or rather was delivered at the shore of Aeolus' kingdom, in a miserable condition, since his stupid men, taken by curiosity, had opened the bag previously given to Odysseus by hospitable Aeolus. The winds came out and a terrible storm destroyed the hero's ship. He had no choice, but to go, shamefully, to Aeolus once more and ask for help. The answer of the King of Winds seems to be shocking (Od. 10. 72-74):

'ἔρρ' ἐκ νήσου θᾶσσον, ἐλέγχιστε ζωόντων;
οὐ γάρ μοι θέμις ἐστὶ κομιζέμεν οὐδ' ἀποπέμπειν
ἄνδρα τόν, ὅς τε θεοῖσιν ἀπέχθηται μακάρεσσιν.

Begone from our island with speed, thou vilest of all that live. In no wise way I help or send upon his way that man who is hated by the blessed god.[75]

A. T. Murray's translation does not show the point: for Aeolus it is not θέμις to help someone who is not dear to the gods. Both helping and send-

---

[74] V. E h r e n b e r g, *op.cit.*, p. 17.

[75] Transl. A. T. M u r r a y, *op.cit.*, vol. I, p. 363; in the edition revised by G. E. D i m o c k, (LOEB, Cambridge, Massachusetts, London, England 1995) the translation is more distinct, but, in our opinion too subjective, because the expression; οὐ θέμις ἐστι is translated as "against all religion".

ing away the stranger were a part of the host's duties.[76] However, a misfortune pressing a man could indicate the wrath of a deity, and in such a case the host was not only free from his duties, but it was not meet to perform them, since it would be against divine will. Of course, it is still open to question on what grounds one could decide that a man coming and asking for help was hated by the gods. Most of men in need had suffered a lot. Aeolus, however, is immortal himself and perhaps his intuition goes much further, than that of other people. What is interesting in this particular adventure is the violation of the most clear and distinct of all the rules of Homeric world: the law of hospitality. In fact, there is no violation at all, and this example shows that θέμις was to a great extent a matter of intuition and wisdom, supported by one's background and piety. A member of Homeric society understood what it meant and this knowledge decided about his social identity.

---

[76] Od. 24. 284-286: εἰ γάρ μιν ζωόν γε κίχεις Ἰθάκης ἐνὶ δήμῳ,
τῶ κέν σ’ εὖ δώροισιν ἀμειψάμενος ἀπέπεμψε
καὶ ξενίῃ ἀγαθῇ· ἡ γὰρ θέμις, ὅς τις ὑπάρξῃ.

Hesiod - δίκη and θέμις in "Theogony" and "Works and Days"

The second of the Greek early epic poets, whose name together with the name of Homer marks the beginning of Greek literature, lived in the end of the 8th century and the first decades of the 7th. It is impossible to indicate the exact period of his life. The similarity of language connecting his poetry with the works of Homer makes it clear that Hesiod worked not too long after the generation of the "Odyssey". There is even a hypothesis according to which the author of the "Iliad" and "Odyssey" was younger[1], but most authors accept the version given above.[2]

Hesiod of Ascra in Beocia is believed to have come to the Greek main land from Cyme in Asia Minor. The poet himself says that his father had to emigrate to seek a better life and run from the poverty and hunger.[3] Perhaps, the pessimistic picture of human life and his attitude towards the world were partly caused by the fact that he had not accepted his new home and did not feel good in this land[4]: *οἰζυρῇ ἐνὶ κώμῃ, Ασκρῃ, χεῖμα κακῇ, θέρει αργαλέη, οὐδέ ποτ' ἐσθλῇ*, in a miserable hamlet, Ascra, which is bad in winter, sultry in summer, and good at no time.[5]

---

[1] This hypothesis was discussed in the excellent commentary written by M. L. W e s t, see: Hesiod, *Theogony*, ed. by M. L. West, London 1965.

[2] For example: M. L. W e s t, *op.cit.*, J. Ł a n o w s k i (introduction to his translation of the Hesiod poetry, *Narodziny bogów (Theogonia), Prace i dni, Tracza*, Warszawa 1999), A. K r o k i e w i c z (*Moralność Homera i etyka Hezjoda*, Warszawa1959), H. L o y d - J o n e s (*The Justice of Zeus*, Berkeley-Los Angeles-London 1971), L. P e a r s o n (*Popular Ethics in Ancient Greece*, Stanford 1960), W. N e s t l e (*Greichiesche Geistesgeschichte*, Stuttgart 1944), E. A. H a v e l o c k (*The Greek Concept of Justice*, Cambridge Mass.-London 1978), H. F r a e n k e l (*Early Greek Poetry and Philosophy*, Oxford 1975). R. M. R o s e n, *Homer and Hesiod*, [in:] *A New Companion to Homer*, ed. by I. Morris and B. Powell, Leiden-New York-Köln 1997, pp. 463 – 487. The arguments supporting the generally accepted view according to which Homeric epics are prior to the Hesiod's poetry will be demonstrated later during discussing the particular passages of the text.

[3] Hesiod, *Works and Days*, 635 ff.

[4] W. J a e g e r, *Paideia*, Warszawa 1964, I, pp. 99-100; Jaeger suggests that, since Hesiod had travelled through the sea only once and gave us the information about this journey (destination was Eubea), he must have been born in Beotia.

[5] *Ibidem* 639-640, translation: H. G. Evelyn-White, M.A., *Hesiod. The Homeric Hymns and Homerica*, LOEB Classical Library, Harvard 1959, p. 51.

He could have a little different background and, perhaps, slightly better education than his fellow country men and it could have been the reason why he felt a little alienated. The poetic craft, the gift of the Muses, made him the poet with the mission to fulfil and this destiny did not make his life easier, although it became the reason for immense pride.

Even if the poetry of Hesiod in the sphere of language and artistic expression is dependable on Homeric epics, and the composition of his works does not have the precision and inner coherence of a masterpiece[6], it is hard to overestimate the significance of Hesiod for the development of literature and ethics. The importance of this poetry consists not in its pure artistic value, but rather in the attitude and views of its author. The very first thought that comes to one's mind is that Hesiod is the first Greek author whose identity is unquestionable. Moreover, he is the first who gives up the anonymity of epic rhapsodos.[7] He steps out as a poet and an author and speaks about his work. Hesiod is not only the first tangible personality in Greek literature, but the first man who follows some definite aims with full conscience.[8] Homer became a teacher, although he did not express his will to be one, whereas, from the beginning, Hesiod appears a mentor, i. e., as one who speaks as an authority. This comes as no surprise when we consider the attitude of both poets towards the Muses: Homer addresses the goddess (he uses the singular) in a conventional invocation, and asks for help. The request is repeated a few times, but shows nothing more than a belief that this is the deity who offers the gift of singing to a poet and helps him to perform. On the other hand, Hesiod describes the whole meeting with the Muses who give him the talent and instruct him that they can tell lies as well as the truth.[9] The last sentence can be understood as a

---

[6] Most authors mentioned above try to find some coherence in the Hesiodic poetry and usually claim that it cannot be compared with Homer directly just because it is different in kind and character, it was composed for different purposes and recited in different circles.

[7] He was probably one of them himself, see; W. J a e g e r, op.cit., p. 91. At least, is is believed that teh beginning of his career was connected with reciting the traditional epic poetry, although it was not his only occupation: he was a farmer.

[8] W. N e s t l e, op.cit., p. 33: "ein Mann, der in hellstem Bewusstsein mit seiner Dichtung ganz bestimmte Zwecke verfolgt. Er will nicht, wie Homer, unterhalten, sondern belehren".

[9] Theog. 22-35. The similarity of this scene to the scenes of theophanies in other religions was discussed by M. L. West (op.cit.), but we can mention the most important elements resembling the scenes from the Old Testament are: the time: night, the position of a chosen man: a shepherd, a place: a mountain Heliocon, a wilderness, where a man is alone, the action of the deity: they *breathed into me a divine voice to celebrate things that shall be and things that were aforetime* (transl. H. G. Evelyn-White): ἐνέπνευσαν δέ μοι αὐδὴν θέσπιν, ἵνα κλείοιμι τά τ᾽ ἐσσομενα πρό τ᾽ ἐόντα. The image reminds us of the scenes described in the lives of Old Testament prophets, although Hesiod was not able to find it out.

discussion with Homer: Hesiod, in contrast to the author of the "Iliad" and "Odyssey", is going to tell the truth. He is given "the better part" of Muses' gift.

There is no doubt that Hesiod treats his poetry very seriously. He is fully aware of the fact that his work can have a strong influence on the listeners' lives.[10] It is still open to discussion whether he mainly gathered and systematized the ideas already present in the mentality, or whether he invented most of them?

The answer for such formulated question is not an easy one. Perhaps, the problem should be put in a different way: to what extent Hesiodic poetry is genuine in the dealing with ideas and problems already present in popular mentality. The poet need not to invent everything in order to be creative. The role of a teacher sometimes consists in awakening human ideas and making people understand what these ideas mean.

There are scholars who claim that it was Hesiod who introduced the idea of justice[11] and became the first moralist.[12] On the other hand, there are interpretations according to which the ideas presented by Hesiod can be already traced in the works of Homer.[13] We believe the second sentence is more correct, but one should remember that we owe the poet of Ascra the development of the idea of justice and its change into an abstract concept.

The world in which Hesiod lived must have been a little similar to the world of the "Odyssey". The picture offered by Homer in his later epic is not entirely realistic, nevertheless, the basic features of the 8th century B. C. were probably preserved in the poetic vision. This is the world where *polis* had not become the central element of society life. In the world of Homer, there are *poleis*, but the city life, so characteristic for the Greek history, is not the dominating way of life. As a matter of fact, a Homeric city resembles a village in many respects. There is a place of meetings and temples, but, for instance, the house of Odysseus, situated in the city, looks more like a manor in the country. The city, *polis,* is the only place to in-

---

This is the task of the anthropology to explain why people living in different times and cultures tend to imagine some exceptional events in the same manner.

[10] H. F r a e n k e l, *op.cit.*, p. 96.

[11] For instance: W. Jaeger, Wilamowitz.

[12] In the opinion of some scholars, the poetry of Hesiod constitutes the real beginning of Greek philosophy; O. Gigon stresses the fact of the novelty of Hesiods invention; the work of the poet belongs to the tradition of Homer due to its epic form, at the same time the aim of the "Theogony" and "Works and Days" sets them apart from the Homeric style and contents; see: O. G i g o n; *Der Ursprung der griechischen Philosophie,* Basel 1968, pp. 13-17.

[13] L. P e a r s o n, *op.cit.,* p. 66 ff, E. A. H a v e l o c k, *op.cit.*, pp. 193-217.

habit, since a village is not mentioned at all. The specific character of Homeric poetry suggests that he had no particular interest in describing country life. The epic poetry of Homer belonged to the sphere of aristocratic culture. It developed as the entertainment for the knights who used to have poets, rhapsodos, i. e. professional performers, in their courts. The archaic culture was still bound to a world of a village and to the life of a peasant family. A village was not opposed to a city, and a farmer was not a symbol of an uneducated man. The court of an aristocrat remained a source of culture, but even in the "Odyssey" we could see that the customs and ideas of aristocracy penetrated the lives of their subjects.[14]

The world of Hesiod is much more realistic. In his works, there is a strange contradiction of the subject and the language. It can be seen especially in the "Works and Days", because the Homeric expressions describe the life and work of a farmer. This bare fact proves that the epic poetry was popular not only among the higher class, but was generally well known. We could say that it modelled the views of all the members of the society. The level of such education must have been relatively high, if a poor farmer like Hesiod was able to compose such a good poetry and take part in poetic contests. Even the fact that he chose poetry as the means of persuading his fellows to live in accord with justice proves that he could count on listeners among his own class. There is no doubt that he addresses the farmers and the so called "ordinary people" in the first place. His attitude towards aristocrats demonstrates that the members of lower classes felt relatively free and were allowed to criticize the rulers. The words of admonition that can be found in both poems, prove not only Hesiod's personal moral standard and courage, but also show that in the society where he lived the freedom of speech must have been recognised at least in some situations.

The next basic statement that should be made about Hesiod's poetry is that these works, though they are written[15] with Homeric words, do not propagate the ideas of their predecessors. Hesiod transforms the ideas known already from Homer, develops them and presents his own model: the ideal of the rural life full of hard work and decent efforts. The ἀρετή, the virtue, of a farmer is far away from the competitive excellence estimated by the heroes of the "Iliad" and "Odyssey".[16] The virtue glorified by Hesiod be-

---

[14] W. J a e g e r, *op.cit.*, p. 89 ff. Jaeger emphasises the fact that the lower classes did not just take the ready patterns from the mightier ones; every social stratum participated in the process of creating ideas and models of life.

[15] The verb is used figuratively; the poetry of Hesiod belongs to the oral culture, and it is not certain whether he actually wrote it. See: A. E. H a v e l o c k, *op.cit.*, pp. 193-194.

[16] The competitive and cooperative virtues were expressions created by A. W. H.

longs to the different world; the poet builds his moral theory in opposition to the aristocratic code.[17] The image of the world and the ideology presented by Hesiod introduced into the Greek culture new values and new mentality: the views of a farmer. Even in the "Theogony" the way of thinking and the choice of the myths points at the character of the author: the world of the immortal gods does not resemble the aristocratic court. The divine world is subjected to the hierarchy and ruled by the will of one strong king, Zeus. Although Hesiod demonstrates his deep respect for the human work, i. e. the work of a farmer, the existence of work in human life is explained in the terms of punishment due to the impudent acts of Prometheus. The gods of Hesiod do not have any special favourites, they do not take care of the people dear to their hearts, they rule and their might is usually associated with the hard lot of the mortals. The next element different from the epic tradition is the realistic and sour picture of women, far from the Homeric courtesy.[18] In the Hesiodic poetry, a woman was sent to men as a disaster. Her presence causes nothing but trouble and is responsible for most miseries in the life of a poor peasant. It is quite clear that these words were written by someone for whom the value of a human, as well as that of an animal or an object, was equal to his or her usefulness in work. Any other qualities could not gain the poet's esteem. This is a way of thinking typical for the farmers whose lives are strictly subjected to hard work and who do not have too much time to enjoy the pleasures of the world (provided that any pleasures can be found in this corrupted world).

The pessimistic image of the world acquired its strongest expression in the myth of five generations.[19] The main rule of human history is deterio-

---

A d k i n s in his famous book: *From the Many to the One*, London 1960 and *Merit and Responsibility*, Oxford 1960. He proves that in the world of Homeric "Iliad" a man does not need to have any peaceful virtues that can be profitable to the community (so called co-operative excellences) in order to be called ἀγαθός, *good*, the translation does not indicate that, in the language of Homer, it is the adjective expressing the highest approval. See: *Merit and Responsibility*, 37 ff. For the analysis of ἀγαθός see also: R. T u r a s i e w i c z, *Studia nad pojęciem "kalos kagathos"*, Warszawa-Kraków 1980.

[17] W. J a e g e r, *op.cit.*, p. 90 ff.

[18] *Ibidem.*

[19] The Works and Days, 109-201. On the other hand, it is worth emphasising that Hesiod shows a great respect for the generations of the heroes which is supposed to be precedent to his own period. This can also explain the change of ideas and general view of the world: Homeric ideals were appropriate for the super-humans who were already dead and left no traces except for the memory of their magnificent deeds. The present generation need another guidance and other ideals. Its destiny is hard life and struggle for everyday bread. The fairy tale is over, the reality has its own necessities. The pessimism of Hesiodic poetry id stressed also by M. Eliade who seas it as the element of the whole Greek religion which

ration. The overwhelming pessimism of this image is lessened by the belief in almighty Zeus who is the guardian of justice and who will eventually award the honest men and punish those who are unjust. Thus, the terms of justice become crucial for proper understanding of Hesiod's poetry, and, *vice versa*, it is impossible to understand what justice meant for Hesiod without considering the image of the world presented in his poems.

"Theogony".

In the poetry of Hesiod, the two well-known terms, δίκη and θέμις, acquire a more uniform meaning. The variety of senses presents by Homeric epics is replaced by the condensed meaning comprising the most important aspects of the term that would be crucial in the future. The significant fact is that the first of the two notions becomes much more popular, the second is rare. It is the symptom of a new period in the development the vocabulary connected with the social norms and law. The semantic range of θέμις is gradually included into the sphere of δίκη.[20] Furthermore, δίκη from the direct expression of divine, then royal, will became the general indication that something should or should not be done. The justice of the *polis* heading towards democracy should be expressed by δίκη rather than θέμις, although both terms remained in the vocabulary. However, δίκη united religious, ethical and political aspects of Greek thought in much greater degree than θέμις.[21] But this was going to happen in the future.

The beginning of this process can be seen in Hesiod. Both terms are used in abstract and concrete meanings, but the difference between Homer and Hesiod consists in the fact that the author of the "Theogony" seems to be fully aware of this fact.

The composition of the "Theogony" has often been criticized. F. M. Cornford quotes the sentence of prof. Mazon who described the earlier Hesiodic poem as "genealogy interrupted by episodes".[22] F. M. Cornford

---

as compared to the judeo-christian tradition seems to be very pessimistic. See: M. E l i a d e, *Historia wierzeń i idei religijnych*, Warszawa 1988, I, pp. 183-185.

[20] Later on, it will be partly replaced by the notion of πρέπον meaning "what is fitting, right". This new term will denote the norm, not necessarily codified, but very important and obeyed by people who called themselves educated and cultural. In the sphere of unwritten rules governing human behaviour πρέπον will take place of θέμις. The latter will remain the old-fashioned and solemn word for "a law". J. W. J o n e s, *The Law and Legal Thery of the Greeks*, Aalen 1977, p. 31 ff, V. E h r e n b e r g, *Die Rechtsidee in frühen Griechentum*, Leipzig 1921, R. H i r z e l, *Themis, Dike, und Vervandtes*, Hildesheim 1966.

[21] J. W. J o n e s, *op.cit.*, p. 31ff.

[22] F. M. C o r n f o r d, *A Ritual Basis for Hesiod's Theogony*, in: *The Unwritten Philosophy and Other Essays*, Cambridge 1967, pp. 95-116.

in his essay proves that the narrative parts of the "Theogony" "fit into the pattern of a very old myth of Creation, known to us from eastern sources and ultimately based on ritual".[23] The poem is planned according to the following pattern: 1) theogony proper; 2) cosmogony, formation of the physical world; 3) the story of the youngest generation of the immortals, led by Zeus, and their struggle to possess Olympus and the supreme power.[24]

In the "Theogony", the name of the goddess Themis (Θέμις) appears for the first time in the line 16 together with the names of the other deities about whom the Muses sing their songs. They praise Zeus, Hera, Athene, Apollo, Artemis, poseidon and "reverend Themis"[25], Θέμιν αἰδοίην, and Aphrodite. The two last names are mentioned together. It is worth remembering that the name of Themis is placed among the most important deities. That proves the significance of the goddess, though there is no explanation referring to her authority; there is no place for that in these lines. The only thing that points at the prerogatives of this goddess is the epithet αἰδοίη, i. e. full of shame. This adjective comes from the noun αἰδώς (aidos), one of the most important Greek terms expressing morals.[26] Αἰδώς, shame, denotes the feeling which prevents a man from committing wrong deeds.[27] The adjective can be understood as "one who deserves respect" and "one who follows αἰδώς". In our opinion, both these senses could be traced in the expression: Θέμις αἰδοίη: the goddess who is connected with αἰδώς deserves the respect. The relation binding Themis and αἰδώς becmes more distinct in the next passages of the poem. Now, there is one more aspect

---

[23] *Ibidem*, p. 95 ff.

[24] *Ibidem*: the cosmology presented by Hesiod follows the pattern known also from the Orphic cosmogonies and Ionian philosophy (from Anaximander). The myth of creation has its counterparts in the Hebrew religion while the rational reflection of the mythical hymn to Zeus comprised in the cosmogony resembles the Genesis and the myth of Marduk. The motif of the king-god slaying the dragon which was the initial act of creation is supposed to belong to the dramatic ritual of the New Year festival. The purpose of this rite was to renovate and recreate the life of a social group and the life of nature. The king became the embodiment of divine power that maintains the living world and the personification of his people. His task was to maintain order and the prosperity of the people depended on the king's righteousness, the Hebrew *Sedek*, Greek δίκη.

[25] Transl. H. G. Evelyn-White, *op.cit.*, p. 79.

[26] There are at least two recent surveys analysing the subject: the thorough and brilliant work of D. L. C a i r n e s, *Aidos. The Psychology and Ethics of Honour and Shame in Ancient Greek Literature*, Oxford 1993, and the very interesting book by B. W i l i a m s, *Shame and necessity*, Berkeley-Los Angeles-Oxford 1993.

[27] The notion of αἰδώς itself is of minor importance in the Hesiodic poetry, nevertheless, its connection with δίκη that becomes ibvious in the "Works and Days" cannot be overlooked; see: D. L. C a i r n e s, *op.cit.*, p. 149 ff.

that should be stressed: Themis is mentioned among the Olympians, not among the elder generation of deities, Tytans, who are spoken of in the subsequent lines and to whom Themis belongs by birth. It may be not intention of the poet, but the position of Themis is really exceptional. In the line 135 we find out that she is a daughter of Uranos (Heaven) and Gaia (Earth).[28] We could infer from the text that she is one of the deities who personify the forces governing the world like her brother Oceanus, or her sister Mnemosyne (Memory). In the next and last passage where the name of Themis is mentioned, it turns out that is became the second, after Metis, wife of Zeus and bore several children; Theog. 901-907:

δεύτερον ἠγάγετο λιπαρὴν Θέμιν, ἣ τέκεν Ὥρας,
Εὐνομίην τε Δίκην τε καὶ Εἰρήνην τεθαλυῖαν,
αἵ τ' ἔργ' ὠρεύουσι καταθνητοῖσι βροτοῖσι,
Μοίρας θ', ἧς πλείστην τιμὴν πόρε μητίετα Ζεύς,
Κλωθώ τε Λάχεσίν τε καὶ Ἄτροπον, αἵ τε διδοῦσι
θνητοῖς ἀνθρώποισιν ἔχειν ἀγαθόν τε κακόν τε.

Second he married sleek Themis, whobore the Watchers, Lawfulness, Justice, and flourishing Peace, who watch over the works of mortal men; and the Fates, to whom Zeus the resourceful gave the most privilege, Clotho, Lachesis, and Atropos, who give mortal men both good and ill.[29]

It seems important to notice that the marriages of Zeus who becomes the king and the ruler of gods and mortal men deserve a particular attention: his first wife, Metis, who was the wisest among gods and mortal men, was swallowed by him.[30] The picture is symbolic: Zeus swallows Metis, Μῆτις, the personification of wisdom.[31] His next move is to marry Themis and to

---

[28] Theog. 132-136:   αὐτὰρ ἔπειτα
Οὐρανῷ εὐνηθεῖσα τέκ' Ὠκεανὸν βαθυδίνην
Κοῖόν τε Κρεῖόν θ' Ὑπερίονά τή Ἰαπετόν τε
Θείαν τε Ῥείαν τε Θέμιν τε Μνημοσύνην τε
Φοίβην τε χρυσοστέφανον Τηθύν τ' ἐρατεινήν.
But afterwords she (Earth) lay with Heaven and bare deep-swirling Oceanus, Coeus and Crius and Hyperion and Iapetus, Theia and Rhea, Themis and Mnemosyne and gold-crowned Phoebe and lovely Thetys - transl. H. G. Evelyn-White, *op.cit.*, p. 89.

[29] Transl. M. L. W e s t, see: Hesiod, *Theogony. Works and Days, A New Translation by M. L. West*, Oxford 1999 (first edition 1988), p. 29.

[30] Hesiod explains that Zeus did it because he was advised so by Earth and Heaven who had warned him that the children of wise Metis could be mightier than their father. The result of this marriage was Athene. Theog. 886-901.

[31] A. Krokiewicz suggests that two female deities, Metis and Themis, could develop from the traces of the very old tradition of the sovereign female goddess worshipped in Peloponnesos and Crete. A. K r o k i e w i c z, *op.cit.*, p. 225.

have children whose task is to rule and bring order into the life of the world: time order and justice together with fate and death are to govern human life in the first place. The next marriages of Zeus are the beginning of the three Graces (with Eurynome as a mother), Persephone (mother: Demeter) and the Muses (born by Mnemosyne). The roles played by these deities could be explained as referring to the following spheres of human existence: beauty, natural vegetation and cultivation of land, and creation (the creative activity of human mind, like poetry).[32]

Such an understanding could be treated as too far fetched, but it is tempting to look at the problem from that point of view.[33]

The peculiar thing is that Themis in the "Theogony" is still a little mysterious character: V. Ehenberg emphasises the fact that in the beginning she is mentioned apart from the Tytans, then she is enumerated as one of this generation, and, finally, described as Zeus' spouse.[34]

The comparison with Homeric poetry reveals no direct connection: Themis, mentioned only three times in the epic (Il. 15. 87, 20. 4; Od. 2. 68), is the deity present in the Olympus (in the "Iliad") and serving Zeus, then, in the "Odyssey", he is called as a goddess of public gatherings. There is no hint referring to her origin and, as it has already been pointed out, there is no reference to the cult of Themis as a chtonic goddess. In the "Theogony", Themis gains new features, her origin is known, but her authority and prerogatives remain obscure. The most distinct element linking the Hesiodic Themis with Homer is the adjective $\lambda\iota\pi\alpha\rho\delta\varsigma$ used in the "Theogony" to describe the goddess. In the "Iliad" this epithet appears together with $\theta\epsilon\mu\iota\sigma\tau\epsilon\varsigma$ in the book 9 (Il. 9. 154, 298)[35] and regards the "decisions that bring profit". The exact meaning of $\lambda\iota\pi\alpha\rho\delta\varsigma$ is "oily, shining", and refers to the positive results of ordinances of a king. In this passage, this is Achilles

---

[32] V. E h r e n b e r g claims that there is no proof that the idea of order is comprised in the notion of Themis and her relationship with Zeus. Such an interpretation is due to the knowledge about Themis and other nemes mentioned in this passage coming from the later sources. In the opinion of this eminent scholar, Themis in the 'Theogonia" has nothing to do with the order of nature. See: V. E h r e n b e r g, *op.cit.*, p. 23 ff.

[33] W. J a e g e r claims that Dike, Eunomia ans Eirene are placed together with Moiras and Charities because of the personal attitude of Hesiod who brought the idea of Dike from his home land in Asia Minor. For him, the three goddesses take care of human work. W. J a e g e r, *op.cit*, pp. 99-100.

[34] *Ibidem.*

[35] we find this expression in the words of Agamemnon's promise. A king is trying to apologise Achilleua and offers him his daughter and seven cities over which Achilleus could rule with "profit-bringing ordinances". For the more detailed analysis, see: the chapter "$\Theta\epsilon\mu\iota\varsigma$ in the "Iliad". The similarity was also noticed by M. L. West, Commentary to Hesiod's *Theogony,* Oxford 1971, 406.

who would be the good ruler bringing profitable ordinances to his people. The fact that Hesiod used this adjective cannot be a coincidence; Themis, as goddess, also brings profit to the world, as it will be shown in the next poem, where Hesiod persuades that living in accord with justice and law make human existence really successful.

The noun θέμις and its plural form θέμιστες, in the "Theogny, appear three times: Theog. 85, 235, 396.

The first passage, Theog. 80-86, refers to the Muses: the most important of them is Calliope:

ἡ γὰρ καὶ βασιλεῦσιν ἅμ' αἰδοίοισιν ὀπηδεῖ.
ὅντινα τιμήσουσι Διὸς κοῦραι μεγάλοιο
γεινόμενόν τε ἴδωσι διοτρεφέων βασιλήων,
τῷ μὲν ἐπὶ γλώσσῃ γλυκερὴν χείουσιν ἐέρσην,
τοῦ δ' ἔπε' ἐκ στόματος ῥεῖ μείλιχα; οἱ δέ νυ λαοὶ
πάντες ἐς αὐτὸν ὁρῶσι διακρίνοντα θέμιστας
ἰθείῃσι δίκῃσιν· ὁ δ' ἀσφαλέως ἀγορεύων
αἶψά τι καὶ μέγα νεῖκος ἐπισταμένως κατέπαυσε

for she attends on worshipful princes: whomsoever of heaven-nourished princes the daughters of great Zeus honour, and behold him at his birth, they pour sweet dew upon his tongue, and from his lips flow gracious words. All the people look towards him while he settles causes with true judgements: even of a great quarrel.[36]

(M. L. West's translation: *and the peoples all look at him as he decides what is to prevail with his straight judgements*).[37]

The protection of the Muses make kings wise and able to guide their folk in a good way.

The passage is worth remembering for the fact that Hesiod ascribes to the Muses the authority going far beyond the task traditionally attributed to them. The Muses of Hesiod give not only the poetic craft and beautiful words, they send wisdom and knowledge haw to judge in a right way and how to settle the arguments. This is why the kings are respected by the people and this is the great and holy gift of the deities to men.[38]

For the purpose of this survey, the most important words in the passage are: διακρίνειν θέμιστας ἰθείῃσι δίκῃσιν. The meaning of θέμιστας is not entirely clear, although the essence of the whole phrase is rather distinct: to

[36] Transl. H. G. Evelyn-White, *op.cit.*, p. 85.
[37] M.L. W e s t, *op.cit.*, p. 5.
[38] Theog. 93: τοίη Μουσάων ἱερὴ δόσις ἀνθρώποισιν.

judge with right judgements. The θέμιστες could denote cases, but this term was associated not with the case, but the decision solving the problem. There is no other possibility but to assume that we should translate the two words together: διακρίνειν θέμιστας as "to judge, to decide in the case", and ἰθείῃσι δίκῃσι as "(rendering) right judgements" The collocation: ἰθείαι δίκαι is known from Homer and means "straight (literal translation of the adjective) judgement". The new translation by M. L. West seems to broaden the sense of the phrase, although this interpretation does not necessarily contradicts the version presumed above. Both the terms, θέμιστες and δίκαι, belong to the sphere of royal authority, like it was in Homer. On the other hand, the context suggests that the power of a king should be treated as a sort of a duty performed in the interest of the people. Furthermore, the gift of the Muses that makes this activity profitable is not offered exclusively to the kings, but "to men". It may be even inferred from that text, that kings, βασιλεῖς, mentioned in these lines and described with the traditional Homeric epithet as διοτρεφοί, nourished by Zeus, could be the special officers, not necessarily the kings. The Greek tradition preserved the title βασιλεύς, though the monarchy in the strict sense was bygone. Certainly, the time of Hesiod was still closer to the world depicted in the "Odyssey" than to the Athenian democratic state. Nevertheless, the kings of the "Odyssey" are not absolute monarchs. The title is used by all the aristocrats and refers just to the social position, and power connected to it, but should not be understood as the name denoting someone similar to a European king in the Middle Ages. The adjective seems to be quite formal and, in our opinion, does not have the same significance as it used to have in the "Iliad", where Zeus' connection with mortal kings had all the features of real and important relationship.[39]

The second passage, Theog. 233-236, refers to Nereus, the eldest son of Pontos, Sea:

Νηρέα δ' ἀψευδέα καὶ ἀληθέα γείνατο Πόντος
πρεσβύτατον παίδων; αὐτὰρ καλέουσι γέροντα,
οὕνεκα νημερτής τε καὶ ἤπιος, οὐδὲ θεμίστων
λήθεται, ἀλλὰ δίκαια καὶ ἤπια δήνεα οἶδεν

And Sea begat Nereus, the eldest of his children, who is true and lies not: and men call him the Old Man because he is trusty and gentle and does not forget the laws of righteousness (M. L. West: does not neglect

---

[39] In the "Odyssey", the meaning of this epithet becomes more formal and traditional, it loses a part of its strength and resembles the expression in Hesiod.

what is right[40]), but thinks just and kindly thoughts.[41]

The image of mild and gentle Nereus differs from the other pictures of the Immortals presented in the poem; there is no other so peaceful and kind a deity in the whole story where the gods fight for power and do it without the shade of mercy. The English translation is very distinct: θέμιστες, in plural, as usually denote concrete, not abstract meaning; this term describes the laws not in the strict sense, as a codified rule, but rather the customary law, a rule of conduct, the notion describing what is right in particular circumstances. This meaning of θέμιστες could already be found in the "Odyssey". Although in this passage, in the background we might feel the abstract principle which will be demonstrated in the "Works and Days". Also, the expression δίκαια δήνεα εἰδέναι, to know just thoughts, points at the abstraction: the adjective δίκαιος for the first time regards the activity of a mind. In Homeric epic, it was a man or his deed that could deserve this epithet that described someone knowing what is the due of a stranger, as well as how to follow someone's δίκη, i. e. his, or her right.

There is one more aspect that can be easily felt in the meaning of δίκαιος and θέμιστες in this passage, although there is no connection between these two terms, that is: absence of violence. This element of the meaning of δίκαιος was already present in the "Iliad"[42], here, it hard not to associate it with Nereus whose kindness and mild heart make him special among other deities.

In the line 396 we come across the well-known expression: ἧ θέμις ἐστίν, as it is right, as it is fitting. This time it refers to the action of Zeus himself; he declares that the deities who had no office under the rule of Cronos, now, after the victory of Zeus, should be raised to "office and rights" , τιμῆς καὶ γεράων.[43] The only new element is that the expression is used to evaluate the divine action, whereas in Homer, it was usually referred to the human behaviour.

In the next passage, among the deities who preserved their position and even gained new authority, Hesiod dedicates a long section to Hecate. He attributes to the daughter of Asteria the particular powers given by Zeus who praised Hecate above the others.[44]

---

[40] M. L. W e s t, *op.cit.*, p. 10.
[41] Transl. H. G. Evelyn-White, *op.cit.*, p. 97.
[42] Il. 11. 832; 13. 6: the epithet describe Cheiron and Abioi.
[43] Theog. 395-396.
[44] Theog. 418-452: Hecate was always a particularly respected goddess. Zeus did not

Mortal people worship Hecate in a special way, and she helps them in many different sphere of their lives. Among others, *in the time of judgement she sits beside august kings; in the public gathering the man of her choice shines out among the crowd.*[45] (Theog. 434, 430):

ἔν τε δίκῃ βασιλεῦσι παρ' αἰδοίοισι καθίζει,
ἔν τ' ἀγορῇ λαοῖσι μεταπρέπει, ὅν κ' ἐθέλῃσιν

Δίκη denotes not the judgement, i. e. decision, but the process of giving judgement, i. e. the settlement of the dispute, we are tempted to say: a court.

In the next poem, "Works and Days", there is much more information about the way Hesiod understood this term since the word δίκη appears very often in the first part of the text.

"Works and Days" (*Opera et dies*)

The first thing that strikes us in the Hesiod's second poem is the concentration of δίκη and θέμις in the first 300 lines and an almost absolute absence of these terms in the next 500 verses.[46] As a matter of fact, δίκη and its derivatives are found in the line 9, 36, 39, 124, 158, 190, 192, and then the whole passage 213-285 is devoted to the idea of justice and full of the terms connected with this sphere (the words derived from the root δικ- appear 25 times). Further, δίκη appears only twice: in the lines 334 and 712. Θέμις is almost completely absent; it occurs three times: in the line 9, 137, and 221. The fact of such a sudden disappearance of the term so popular in the "Iliad" and, especially, in the "Odyssey", can be explained in many different ways. It seems to us that one of the possible reasons is that the behaviour of an individual, in the family life as well as in the society, is defined by the legal or proto-legal (not written yet) rules to a greater degree than it used to be in the times of Homer. In the previous period social life was ruled by an unwritten, customary norm, rather intuitively felt than strictly described by the members of the same cultural community. This was generally the norm, or norms, belonging to the aristocratic code, and denoted by the word θέμις.[47]

---

take anything from her, on the contrary, he honoured her with his special favours. A part of Heaven and Sea belongs to her and she sends prosperity to human.

[45] Transl. M. L. W e s t,, *op.cit.*, pp. 15-16.

[46] E. A. Havelock emphasized this feature of Hesiodic poetry and noticed that nothing like this could be found in Homer, yet, as he observed, knowledge of Homeric epic is necessary to understand Hesiod. See: E. A. H a v e l o c k, *op. cit.*, p. 194 ff.

[47] E. Benveniste claims that θέμις refers to the family law (le droit familial), whereas δίκη denotes the law between families in the tribe. See: E. B e n v e n i s t e, *Le Vocabulaire des institutions indo-européennes*, Paris 1969, II, pp. 102-103.

The first passage, where we find both terms, is the invocation. In the line 9, the apostrophe to the Muses does not resemble the traditional beginning of an epic poem; from the second line we know that the real hero of the "Work and Days" is Zeus. The Muses are called to sing about their father whose name appears instead of the name of Odysseus or Achilles (Op.1-2). The vocabulary looks familiar:

Μοῦσαι Πιερίηθεν ἀοιδῆσιν κλείουσαι
δεῦτε, Δί᾽ ἐννέπετε, σφέτερον πατέρ᾽ ὑμνείουσαι;

Muses of Pieria who give glory through song, come hither, tell of Zeus your father and chant his praise[48]

The next lines describe the highest god and explain why, in the eyes of the poet, he deserves so much attention: it is Zeus who sends fame to people, he gives a man strength and takes it back, he also " *easily he makes the crooked straight and withers the proud*"[49], ῥεία δέ τ᾽ ἰθύνει σκολιὸν καὶ γηήνορα κάρφει (Op. 6). Zeus sends good and evil to men, their lot depends on his will, but it becomes obvious that his decisions are connected with human behaviour and could be understood almost as an award or a punishment. The image of Zeus is radically changed as compared to the "Iliad" and, even, although less so, in comparison to the "Odyssey. The invocation ends with a request (to Zeus) and a call to Perses to whom the whole poem is dedicated (Op.9-10):

κλῦθι ἰδὼν ἀίων τε, δίκη δ᾽ ἴθυνε θέμιστας
τύνη; ἐγὼ δέ κε, Πέρση, ἐτήτυμα μυθησαίμην.[50]

Attend thou with eye and ear, and make judgements straight with righteousness. And I, Perses, would tell of true things.[51]

---

[48] Transl. M. L. W e s t, *op.cit.*, p. 37.

[49] *Ibidem.*

[50] The text version in this line is based on the LOEB edition, not on the TLG, as in other passages. The differences are rare, so we can use the LOEB translation (H. G. Evelyn-White), but in this particular line there is a difference: LOEB has Πέρση in the Vocative case, while TLG suggests the Dative: Πέρση. The second version was followed also by J. Ł a n o w s k i in his translation of Hesiod's "Works and Days"; see: Hezjod, *Narodziny Bogów (Theogonia), Prace i dni, Tarcza*, Warszawa 1999, p. 61.

[51] transl. H. G. Evelyn-White, see: *Hesiod, The Homeric Hymns and Homerica*, LOEB Classical Library, Harvard 1959, p. 3; the translation by M. L. West, based on the text his critical edition of The Works and Days (*Works and Days*, 1978): "*O harken as thou seest and hearest, and make judgements straight with righteousness, Lord; while I should like to tell Perses words of truth*", *op.cit.*, p. 37.

The didactic character of the "Works and Days" is visible in the admonishing tendency of this poem. The process regarding the heritage, which ended in favour of Perses and made Hesiod feel unjustly injured was only an excuse to introduce the moral theory whose central part is constituted by Zeus and his authority.[52] The process with Perses was the reason why Hesiod was interested in the ethics. However, in the course of the poem, there is less and less information about this case; we do not even know what was the result of Hesiod's efforts to regain his part of the property. This fact was the reason why some scholars suspected that Hesiod was writing the poem during the process, so he did not know the end of it himself.[53]

The meaning of δίκη in this passage is already associated with an abstract, and the English translation quoted above renders this sense perfectly: with righteousness. Θέμιστες denote the decisions taken in the dispute by someone who is supposed to settle it.

The next passage of a particular interest for this study is Op. 35-39:

ἀλλ' αὖθι διακρινώμεθα νεῖκος
"θείῃσι δίκης, αἵ τ' ἐκ Διός ε"σιν ἄρισται.
ἤδη μὲν γὰρ κλῆρον ἐδασσάμεθ', ἄλλα τε πολλὰ
ἁρπάζων ἐφόρεις μέγα κυδαίνων βασιλῆας
δωροφάγους, οἳ τήνδε δίκην ἐθέλουσι δικάσσαι.

nay, let us settle our dispute with straight judgement, the best that Zeus sends. For we divided our estate before, and you kept grabbing and taking much more, paying great tribute to the lords, those bribe-swallowers, who see fit to make this their judgement.[54]

In his appeal to Perses, Hesiod does not explain the exact cause of the quarrel. It could be one more proof that the process is not the most important subject of the poem. The terms: δίκη and δικάζειν have quite a technical meaning. The first one denotes judgement, a resolution (in the line 36,

---

[52] D. D e m b i ń s k a - S i u r y, *Człowiek odkrywa człowieka.,O początkach greckiej refleksji moralnej*, Warszawa 1991, p. 54 ff: Zeus is supposed to be the highest moral authority and δίκη becomes justice, the basic and universal rule in the world.

[53] W. J a e g e r mentioned such a hypothesis; *op.cit.*, p. 93.

[54] Transl. M. L. W e s t, *op.cit.*, p. 38; translation by H. G. Evelyn-White: *nay, let us settle our dispute here with true judgement which is of Zeus and is perfect. For we had already divided our inheritance, but you seized the greater share and carried it off, greatly swelling the glory of our bribe-swallowing lords who love to judge such a cause as this, op.cit.*, p. 5.

with a characteristic epithet ἰθύς), the second signifies the process of deciding, arriving at a verdict.

Δίκη bares the same meaning in the line 124 where is mentioned as a subject of care for the spirits of men of golden generation, who now *keep watch on judgements and cruel deeds*[55], οἵ ῥα φυλάσσουσίν τε δίκας καὶ σχέτλια ἔργα.

In both passages, Hesiod has no doubt that wrong doings and injustice would be punished. In the line 40, talking about the bribe taking judges[56], he calls them νήπιοι using the famous Homerc adjective that always described fools unaware of the approaching doom.

In the line 137, we come across the expression that used to be popular in Homeric epics, but seldom appears in the works of Hesiod. People of the second generation did not want to serve the gods, or offer sacrifice on the altars *as ii right for men to do wherever they dwell*[57], ᾗ θέμις ἀνθρώποις κατὰ ἤθεα. The expression κατὰ ἤθεα can be understood in two ways: the version of H. G. Evelyn-White renders ἦθος as a place of dwelling, but the second possibility is to translate this word as "custom". The latter fits better into the context, because it can be inferred from the preceding expression: θέμις (ἐστι) ἀνθρώποις.[58]

The adjective δίκαιος in the comparative occurs in the line 158; it describes the next generation, the heroes, ἀνδρῶν ἡρώων θεῖον γένος, who were δικαιότερον καὶ ἄρειον, more righteous and braver. Unfortunately, Hesiod does not provide us with any features that would explain what exactly he meant by the noun δίκαιος.

The lines 189-194 are a part of the description of the present generation, precisely, they are a prophecy: Hesiod expects every possible disaster, since the foolishness and impudence of men tend to grow. He even invents a new noun to describe aggressive deeds of people who do not respect their parents; he calls them χειροδίκαι, men who assert their right by hand, i. e., men who use the right of might[59] (Op. 189).

---

[55] Transl. H. G. Evelyn-White, *op.cit.*, p. 12.

[56] Almost everybody studying Hesiod notices Hesiod's courage in criticizing the judges. It could be a sign of the new social situation: Hesiod, a person to whom the decisions of the rulers and judges, θέμιστες, are addressed, is able to criticise them. It is the best proof that the society has gone a long way since the time and situation described in the "Iliad". Furthermore, the judges are called βασιλεῖς, "kings", but the context suggests that this name could already denote people performing the function of a judge.

[57] Transl. H. G. Evelyn-White, *op.cit.*, p. 13.

[58] The phrase was translated in this way by J. Łanowski, *op.cit.*, p. 64.

[59] See: The Greek-English Lexicon, Liddel-Scott, 1958, p. 1985.

The pessimistic image goes as follows (Op.190-194):

οὐδέ τις εὐόρκου χάρις ἔσσεται οὐδὲ δικαίου
οὐδ᾽ ἀγαθοῦ, μᾶλλον δὲ κακῶν ῥεκτῆρα καὶ ὕβριν
ἀνέρες αἰνήσουσι[60] ῥ δίκη δ᾽ ἐν χερσίρ καὶ αἰδὼς
οὐκ ἔσται, βλάψει δ᾽ ὁ κακὸς τὸν ἀρείονα φῶτα
μύθοισι σκολιοῖς ἐνέπων, ἐπὶ δ᾽ ὅρκον ὀμεῖται.

(...) and there will be no thanks for the man who abides by the oath or for the righteous or wrthy man, but instead they will honour the miscreant and the criminal. Law and decency will be in fists. The villain will do bette down by telling crooked tales, and will swear his oath upon him.[61]

The moralistic sense of this passage can be treated as a prelude to the most important fragment of the poem, i. e. the lines 213-285, where Hesiodic ethic is expressed in one, coherent lecture. We may infer from the context and from the vicinity of the adjective εὔορκος τηατ δίκαιος ανδ ἀγαθός refer to a man and not to the abstraction. Thus, they mean: just and good. In this passage, we find the opposition δίκαιος (δίκη) - ὕβρις, a just (man) - impudence, violence, for the first time. It is going to be crucial in the next lines. The greed, corruption and violence of the men in power become the worst evil of the time.[62] This sad truth is illustrated by the fable about a hawk and a nightingale which plays the role of a prelude to the next passage (Op. 202-212).

The ideas presented by Hesiod sometimes seem to be entirely new; some differences between Hesiod and Homer have already been indicated. Nevertheless, the claim that Hesiod introduced the ideal of justice is rejected by some authorities on the subject[63], who argue that the ideas of Hesiod were taken from >the doctrine of Zeus, justice and the responsibilities of the *basileis,* which can be seen most clearly in the "Odyssey", but which is already present in the "Iliad"<.[64] The analysis of E. A. Havelock also proves that Hesiod based the image of his moral theory on the concepts created by Homer. Generally, these statements are true, but, in our opinion, there is

---

[60] The version accepted by LOEB, *op.cit.*, p. 16; the second possibility: ἀνέρα τιμήσουσι (MSS); M.L. West claims that in this case ὕβριν qualifies ἀνέρα as if it were the adjective ὑβριστήν. He is Hybris incarnate. See: Hesiod, *Works and Days,* edited with Prolegomena and Commentary by M. L. W e s t, Oxford 1982, p. 202.

[61] Transl. M. L. W e s t, *op. cit.* p. 42.

[62] L. Pearson, op.cit, 72; this remark refers not only to Hesiod, but also to Solon and Theognis.

[63] For instance: H. Lloyd-Jones, *op.cit.,* p. 35 ff, E. A. Havelock, *op.cit.,* p. 193 ff.

[64] H. Lloyd-Jones, *ibidem.*

one correction that should be done: Hesiod used the concepts of Homer in order to construct and present his idea of justice, but it was a creative process. He knew Homeric epics, and took from them what was most precious to him and what was not necessarily the most important to Homer. Justice is present in Homeric epic, and it is hard to deny that the concept has just been born and its abstract sense can be felt in the background, but the terms used to describe it have mostly a concrete meaning. This is Hesiod who made the next move and developed the abstract notion of justice. Maybe, he just collected Homer's thoughts concerning the subject and presented them in the form of a lecture. Nevertheless, it was a very important, and maybe, decisive step towards development of the moral theory that was going to be created by the next generations of Greek thinkers. Having in mind these few remarks, we may proceed to the most important passage, Op. 213-284.

The whole passage can be divided into eight parts;[65]
213-219 - ὕβρις versus law,
220-224 - the personification of Justice as an abused woman,
225-237- the life of just men,
238-247- the life of evil-doers,
248-255- appeal to the rulers; guardians of law,
256-262- Justice, the daughter of Zeus,
263-273- second appeal; good advice,
274-285- the last admonition to Perses; the gift of Zeus and his requirements.

Op. 213-219:

> Ὦ Πέρση, σὺ δ' ἄκουε δίκης μηδ' ὕβριν ὄφελλε;
> ὕβρις γάρ τε κακὴ δειλῷ βροτῷ, οὐδὲ μὲν ἐσθλὸς
> ῥηιδίως φερέμεν δύναται, βαρύθει δέ θ' ὑπ' αὐτῆς
> ἐγκύρσας ἄτῃσιν; ὁδὸς δ' ἑτέρηφι παρελθεῖν
> κρείσσων ἐς τὰ δίκαια; δίκη δ' ὑπὲρ ὕβριος ἴσχει
> ἐς τέλος ἐξελθοῦσα; παθὼν δέ τε νήπιος ἔγνω.
> αὐτίκα γὰρ τρέχει Ὅρκος ἅμα σκολιῇσι δίκῃσιν;

Butyou, Perses, must hearken to Right and not promote violence. For violence is bad for a lowly man; not even a man of worth can carry it easily, but he sinks under it when he runs into Blights. The road on the other side gives better passage, to righteousness: Right (transl. By Evelyn-White: Justice) gets the upper hand over violence in the end. The fool learns

---

[65] This division almost corresponds to that made by E. A. H a v e l o c k, *op.cit.*, pp. 195-212.

only by experience. For Oath at once runs level with crooked judgements;[66]

At the very beginning of the passage, we come across the term δίκη. M. L. West remarks that it is always problematic whether it should be written with a small letter or a capital one. This depends on the degree of personification of the notion, but in the poetry of Hesiod the two tendencies (to personify and to not to do so) are freely combined.[67] It is sometimes really impossible to tell which one is correct. Moreover, one is tempted to say that in the same place both the senses could be seen. This is particularly true in the passage mentioned above. On the other hand, whether there is a capital letter in the word δίκη, or not, seems to be of secondary importance, since in both versions the term denotes an abstract idea of righteousness. This term is opposed to hybris (ὕβρις), i.e. violence, outrage, and impudence combined together. We are going to leave this term in the Greek version, since every translation renders only a part of its meaning.[68]

For E. M. Havelock, justice, δίκη, in these lines is equated with non-aggression.[69] That would be the natural development of Homeric concept, but it seems to be something more than non-using violence, though the absence of violence is certainly the most important part of it. The antithesis: justice - hybris is repeated in the following lines. The bad man will fall, even if he is prosperous. West points out that every moral theory has to overcome the problem of evil men doing well. The solution is simple: the punishment comes in the end.[70] The path leading to right things resembles the popular tale of Heracles and the choice between the good and evil way of life, described by Xenophon. Perhaps, this is the source of the concept. Τὰ δίκαια meaning "good, right things", appears quite often in the poetry of Theognis and in a few places in the works of Xenophon.[71] E. A. Havelock notices that in the line 217, the justice from being the destination becomes a competitor in the race. In the line 219, justice and hybris are replaced by an Oath and crooked judgements.[72] The oath here is personified.[73] The

---

[66] Transl. M. L. W e s t, *op.cit.,* p. 43.

[67] M. L. W e s t, see: commentary and prolegomena in: Hesiod, *Works and Days,* ed. by M. L. W e s t, Oxford 1982, p. 210; he assumes Δίκης in the line 213.

[68] For the same solution, see: M.L. West. E. A. Havelock translates it as "outrage" and emphasizes that hybris would become a commonplace notion in the Greek literature after Hesiod; see: E. A. H a v e l o c k, *op.cit.,* p. 195.

[69] E. M. H a v e l o c k, *ibidem.*

[70] M. L. W e s t, commentary on the *"Works and Days",* *op.cit.,* p. 211.

[71] *Ibidem,* p. 210.

[72] E. A. H a v e l o c k, *op.cit.,* p. 196.

[73] M. L. W e s t, *op.cit.,* p. 211: divine sanctions for the litigants committing perjury are mentioned several times in the literature, for instance: Th. 231, Aesch. *Ctes.* 233.

image presented by Hesiod can be associated with the race from the 23rd book of the "Iliad" and the controversy between Menelaus and Antilochos. At least this is the interpretation of E. A. Havelock[74] who emphasizes the similar elements: the narrow street, the bypassing, the foolishness of a young man, and the victory of justice. In Hesiod, the person of Menelaus is replaced by Justice who eventually wins, as the king won in the end.

The composition of the whole fragment shows a sudden change of subject. There is no transition to the next passage, which brings even closer resemblance to Homer:

Op. 220-224:

τῆς δὲ Δίκης ῥόθος ἑλκομένης ἧ κ' ἄνδρες ἄγωσι
δωροφάγοι, σκολιῆς δὲ δίκης κρίνωσι θέμιστας;
ἡ δ' ἕπεται κλαίουσα πόλιν καὶ ἤθεα λαῶν,
ἠέρα ἑσσαμένη, κακὸν ἀνθρώποισι φέρουσα,
οἵ τέ μιν ἐξελάσωσι καὶ οὐκ ἰθεῖαν ἔνειμαν.

There is angry murmuring when Right (transl. Evelyn-White: *Justice*[75]) *is dragged off wherever bribe-swallowers choose to take her as they give judgement with crooked verdicts; and she follows weeping to those people's town and territories clad in darkness, bringing ill to men who drive her out and do not dispense her straight.*[76]

There is no doubt that in this passage Δίκη is a personification. It is presented as a maiden dragged from her path.[77] Justice becomes a woman who does not appear again in these particular circumstances.[78] According to Havelock, the image of an abused woman is not an incidental idea that came to Hesiod's mind. It is based on the well-known pattern. The picture of Justice in the line 220 repeats the story known from the 1st book of the "Iliad" (Il. 1. 29-31). The woman taken somewhere against her will is Chryseis, another example is Breseis. A very similar fate is predicted to Andromache (Il. 6. 454 ff.). In the story of a war, the image of abused women fits into the general outline, nevertheless, at least first two examples are exceptionally important. They tell not only the dramatic story of women's fate, but also show that in these cases, the misfortunes of women

---

[74] E. A. H a v e l o c k, *ibidem.*
[75] Transl. H. G. Evelyn-White, *op.cit.*, p. 19.
[76] Transl. M. L. W e s t, *op.cit.*, p. 43.
[77] M. L. W e s t, *op.cit.*, p. 211, see also: V. E h r e n b e r g, *op.cit.*, pp. 67-69.
[78] E. A. H a v e l o c k, *op.cit.*, pp. 198-201.

bring disasters to the evil-doers. *Both women symbolise in one person justice violated and justice restored.*[79]

There is one more feature that makes us believe that Homer was always the source of inspiration for Hesiod: the girl coming into the town wrapped in mist. The reference can be easily found in the 6th book of the "Odyssey": the hero goes into the city of Phaecians covered with mist. The change of the gender is not so important if we remember that Odysseus is accompanied by two women: Athene and Nausicaa.[80]

Furthermore, when Odysseus secretly comes to another city (in his own land), he is an avenger. Hesiodic expression: κακὸν ἀνθρώποισι φέρουσα, bringing evil to mankind, is the equivalent of the words used in the "Odyssey" (Od. 14. 110; 17. 27; 82, 159; 16. 103; 20. 367-368).[81]

The lines 225-237 present the image of Utopia:

> οἳ δὲ δίκας ξείνοισι καὶ ἐνδήμοισι διδοῦσιν
> ἰθείας καὶ μή τι παρεκβαίνουσι δικαίου,
> τοῖσι τέθηλε πόλις, λαοὶ δ' ἀνθεῦσιν ἐν αὐτῇ;
> εἰρήνη δ' ἀνὰ γῆν κουροτρόφος, οὐδέ ποτ' αὐτοῖς
> ἀργαλέον πόλεμον τεκμαίρεται εὐρύοπα Ζεύς;
> οὐδέ ποτ' ἰθυδίκῃσι μετ' ἀνδράσι λιμὸς ὀπηδεῖ
> οὐδ' ἄτη, θαλίης δὲ μεμηλότα ἔργα νέμονται.
> τοῖσι φέρει μὲν γαῖα πολὺν βίον, οὔρεσι δὲ δρῦς
> ἄκρη μέν τε φέρει βαλάνους, μέσση δὲ μελίσσας;
> εἰροπόκοι δ' ὄιες μαλλοῖς καταβεβρίθασι;
> τίκτουσιν δὲ γυναῖκες ἐοικότα τέκνα γονεῦσι;
> θάλλουσιν δ' ἀγαθοῖσι διαμπερές; οὐδ' ἐπὶ νηῶν
> νίσονται, καρπὸν δὲ φέρει ζείδωρος ἄρουρα.

The picture of a perfect world inhabited by just and honest people reminds us of the first generation of men.[82] The perfect life consists in eternal peace, which provides ideal background for the development of the society: a great many children are born, the gods never decree war against this happy land inhabited by honest people, who do not know any sort of disaster nor famine; their land brings them crops without effort and they do not need to travel abroad. There are, certainly, differences, but we may infer that the image presented in this passage refers to the best possible

---

[79] *Ibidem*, p. 198.
[80] *Ibidem*, p. 200.
[81] *Ibidem*, p. 201.
[82] Noticed also by M. L. W e s t, *op.cit.*, p. 213.

reality. E. A. Havelock points at all the details of this description which are similar to the characteristics of Scheria provided by Homer in the 6th book of the "Odyssey".[83] The magic land of Phaecians was also a peaceful, rich and a little alienated place. Also in Scheria there are handsome κοῦροι, who in Hesiod are nourished by peace.[84] The life in the Hesiodic paradise, like in Scheria. is devoted to pleasure. The agriculture brings fantastic crops in both lands and famine is unknown to the inhabitants of both worlds. The only detail that is different in the two poems refers to the sea and ships; Hesiod was not a sailor and did not regard the sea as the natural environment for a human.

The term δίκη in the line 226 is a little misleading. There is an impression that what Hesiod refers to is the norm of social conduct. Δίκη of a stranger could be an equivalent for δίκη of Achilles ("Iliad", book 9) and of Antilochos ("Iliad", book 23), but the context makes it clear that the correct translation is "judgement". The epithet ἰθεία δίκη used by Hesiod belongs to Homeric language. On the other hand, the meaning of δίκαιος comprises broader sphere than it used to in the poems of Homer.

The description of an Utopia contrasts with the picture of another state, which is supposed to be a negative example. In the lines 238-247 we are given the mirror reflection of the city of Justice. This second state is the victim of hybris. Zeus punishes the whole city even for the wrong deeds (ἀτάσθαλα ἔργα) of one man.[85]

M. L. West claims that the whole passage comparing the two cities, just and unjust, resembles the Semitic images in its conception and content (to compare with *Levit.* 26, *Deut.* 28). The idea of the fertility of the earth and livestock can be found in the "Odyssey", Od. 9. 109 ff.[86]

Δίκη acquires a new sense: a punishment sent by Zeus to those who have hybris in their hearts;

οἷς δ' ὕβρις τε μέμηλε κακὴ καὶ σχέτλια ἔργα,
τοῖς δὲ δίκην Κρονίδης τεκμαίρεται εὐρύοπα Ζεύς.

---

[83] E. A. H a v e l o c k, *op.cit.*, p. 201 ff.

[84] M. L. W e s t: the expression: Εἰρήνη κουρότρεφος is found also in: E. *Ba.* 420, *Supp.* 490; Pind. fr. 109.3 f.

[85] The image of a man bringing a disaster to the whole city can be associated with the concept of pollution, μίασμα, the term which becomes very important in the later literature. See: A. W. H. A d k i n s, *Merit and Responsibility. A Study in Grek Values,* Oxford 1960, pp. 86-115.

[86] M. L. W e s t, *op.cit.*, p. 213.

But for those who practise violence and cruel deeds, far-seeing Zeus, the son of Cronos, ordains a punishment.[87]

Further lines, 248-255, contain some mysterious ideas, namely the mention about the Guardians of Justice. The appeal to the kings is a warning at the same time: *mark well this punishment you also; for the deathless gods are near among men and mark all those who oppress their fellows with crooked judgements, and reck not the anger of the gods;*

Ὦ βασιλῆς, ὑμεῖς δὲ καταφράζεσθε καὶ αὐτοὶ
τήνδε δίκην; ἐγγὺς γὰρ ἐν ἀνθρώποισιν ἐόντες
ἀθάνατοι φράζονται ὅσοι σκολιῇσι δίκῃσιν
ἀλλήλους τρίβουσι θεῶν ὄπιν οὐκ ἀλέγοντες.

Δίκη in the line 248 means "a punishment" and serves as the transition from the previous passage. In the line 250, there are again σκόλιαι δίκαι, crooked judgements.

The warning continues; Hesiod speaks about the guardians of mortal men, φύλακες θνητῶν ἀνθρώπων, whose task is to protect judgements and wrong deeds, δίκας καὶ σχέτλια ἔργα (Op. 253).

There is no explanation who these watchers are, but the most significant fact is that apart from Zeus, there is another source of divine sanction, probably subjected to the highest god, still acting independently.

The next passage is probably the most significant for Hesiod's moral concepts; Op. 256-262:

ἡ δέ τε παρθένος ἐστὶ Δίκη, Διὸς ἐκγεγαυῖα,
κυδρή τ' αἰδοίη τε θεοῖς οἳ Ὄλυμπον ἔχουσιν,
καί ῥ' ὁπότ' ἄν τίς μιν βλάπτῃ σκολιῶς ὀνοτάζων,
αὐτίκα πὰρ Διὶ πατρὶ καθεζομένη Κρονίωνι
γηρύετ' ἀνθρώπων ἀδίκων νόον, ὄφρ' ἀποτείσῃ
δῆμος ἀτασθαλίας βασιλέων οἳ λυγρὰ νοεῦντες
ἄλλῃ παρκλίνωσι δίκας σκολιῶς ἐνέποντες.

And there is that maiden Right, daughter of Zeus, esteemed and respected by the gods in Olympus; and whenever someone does her down with crooked abuse, at once she sits by Zeus her father, Kronos' son, and reports the men's unrighteous mind, so that people may pay for the crimes of their lords who balefully divert justice from its course by pronouncing it crooked.[88]

---

[87] Transl. H. G. Evelyn-White, *op.cit.*, p. 21.
[88] Transl. M. L. W e s t, *op.cit.*, p. 44.

The female goddess with unique a authority, Justice, seems to be Hesiod's genuine invention. However, E. A. Havelock compares her features with the characteristics of Athene from the "Odyssey". The result of his analysis is that both deities have much in common.[89] On the other hand, the dependence on Homer is not of primary importance. The most significant is the distinct and clear concept of a deity who is a personification of δίκη. From the term denoting a concrete, and then a less concrete notion of righteousness, δίκη developed into the word the abstract meaning of which should not be questioned.[90]

The next fragment, 263-285, contains the second appeal to the rulers, good advice for all the men, and a direct appeal to Perses. Then, we come across particularly interesting passage:

Op. 276-281:

τόνδε γὰρ ἀνθρώποισι νόμον διέταξε Κρονίων,
ἰχθύσι μὲν καὶ θηρσὶ καὶ οἰωνοῖς πετεηνοῖς
ἔσθειν ἀλλήλους, ἐπεὶ οὐ δίκη ἐστὶ μετ’ αὐτοῖς;
ἀνθρώποισι δ’ ἔδωκε δίκην, ἣ πολλὸν ἀρίστη
γίνεται; εἰ γάρ τίς κ’ ἐθέλῃ τὰ δίκαι’ ἀγορεῦσαι
γινώσκων, τῷ μέν τ’ ὄλβον διδοῖ εὐρύοπα Ζεύς;

For this was the rule for men that Kronos' son laid down: whereas fish and beasts and flying birds would eat one another, because Right is not among them, to men he have Right (transl. Evelyn-White: *Justice*), *which is much the best in practice. For if a man is willing to say what he knows to be just, to him wide-seeing Zeus gives prosperity;*[91]

Already in Homer δίκη was asociated with non-aggresion and regarded as the criterion of civilization. However, it was supposed to be an element of Greek culture, and there were human, or semi-human, creatures who did not recognise its authority. Hesiod for the first time demonstrates this term as the criterion of being a human, the most crucial element that constitutes the difference between a man and an animal. Δίκη denotes here the right,

---

[89] E. A. H a v e l o c k, *op.cit.*, p. 206 ff.

[90] This claim was criticised by M. Gagarin who tries to demonstrate that in the "Works and Days" this term denotes "a law", a peaceful settlement of the dispute. Apart from the legal meaning, it has no general sense. See: M. G a g a r i n, *Dike in the Works and Days,* Classical Philology 68 (1973): pp. 81-94. His controversial statement was discussed by M. W. D i c k i e, *Dike as a Moral Term in Homer and Hesiod,* Classical Philology 73: pp. 91-101.

[91] Transl. M. L. W e s t, *op.cit.*, p. 45.

the rule of which makes human life possible.[92]

The comparison with Homer is reasonable, but one fact should be emphasised: Hesiod systematised the notions used by Homer and created the moral theory out of single elements.

Hesiod's poetry became not only a moral guidebook for the audience. His ideas regarding the world of nature and people and his conception of Justice as a principle of the world made an impact on the philosophers and contributed to the presocratic theory of cosmos.[93]

The idea of δίκη, justice, understood as the most important factor in human life was partly based on the concepts already present in Homer. Nevertheless, Hesiod changed it into an abstract principle.

The meaning of the word δίκη comprises both abstract and concrete senses. It is sometimes used to denote an idea, but there are many passages where its meaning is concrete and technical: a judgement, a process. The flexibility of the exact sense of this term seems to be a characteristic feature of Hesiodic language. The situation when the abstract and concrete senses are visible in the same word occurs quite often.

---

[92] See: E. A. H a v e l o c k, *op.cit.*, p. 213, D. D e m b i ń s k a – S i u r y, *op.cit.*, L. P e a r s o n, *op.cit.*, p. 72 ff.

[93] For the analysis of this issue see: M. D e t i e n n e, *Homere, Hésiode et Pythagore. Poesie et philosophie dans le pythagorisme ancien,* Bruxelles-Berchem 1962; H. D i l l e r, *Hesiod und die Anfänge der griechischen Philosophie,* Antike und Abendland B. II (1946), pp. 140-151.

Conclusion

The analysis of development of the terms θέμις and δίκη is not an easy task. Both notions were used in many senses. The definition of the exact meaning of these terms turns to be almost impossible. The early Greek literature, represented by Homer, Hesiod and some lyric poets, remains the only source of knowledge regarding the beginning of Greek thought. It is the only way to reveal the picture of the Greek society and its culture in the 9th, 8th, and 7th centuries. One should be very careful while making any statements concerning this period, since the material is far from being complete. Most of theories explaining the meaning of basic notions the significance of which is connected with the development of Greek society are hypotheses based not only on the written sources, but also on the intuition of an author. One may very easily get an impression that many such theories seem rather subjective. The same remark could be referred to this study. Nevertheless, we should try to summarize the content of this work.

Both terms that were the subject of our analysis are regarded as crucial for the history of a society and for the development of a state. Both of them express a norm in a very broad sense, their meaning, however, is slightly different in every work analysed in this survey.

In ·Homeric epics, θέμις appears more often than δίκη. It seems that the first notion played a little more important role in the lives of the people depicted by Homer. In the "Iliad", θέμις used to mean mainly the ordinances of a king and the unwritten norm of behaviour referring the life of a man. The connection with the royal power was emphasised by the divine sanction and was quite natural in the society where a king was the only authority. His decisions were called θέμιστες and were usually applied to the concrete situations. An abstract meaning could be noticed in the background of θέμις denoting the rules of human behaviour. The existence of such norm and its authority was not connected with any written code. The definition of θέμις was encoded in human minds and the decision whether something is in accord with θέμις, or not, depended on the intuition.

The existence of this phenomenon is more distinct in the "Odyssey" where θέμις begins to define the norm of the aristocratic society. The differences between the "Iliad" and the "Odyssey" are due to the fact that the former belongs to the earlier period, the times of monarchy, while the latter expresses rather the ideas of the next stage of social development.

Hesiod took both terms and used them in his own way. His work is close to the world presented in the "Odyssey". However, his definition of $\theta\acute{\epsilon}\mu\iota\varsigma$ seems to be the end of the development of this term. It becomes an abstract, personified in the name of te goddess. After Hesiod, there is not too much to say about this term which is very rare in the works of other poets of the early archaic age.

The disappearance of $\theta\acute{\epsilon}\mu\iota\varsigma$ could be explained by the special character of this notion. It was unwritten norm the meaning of which became smaller in the society ruled by law which more and more often was codified. The new times were the times of $\delta\acute{\iota}\kappa\eta$ which since Hesiod becomes the most important term connected with the development of moral thinking. Even in the works of Homer, this term was not devoid of moral significance, but in the poetry of Hesiod the abstract meaning of $\delta\acute{\iota}\kappa\eta$ as the principle of justice become evident. However, it should be stressed that this term was also used to denote quite concrete things.

All the senses of $\delta\acute{\iota}\kappa\eta$ could be found in the lyric poetry. The most important and most distinct example is the poetry of Solon. In his poems $\delta\acute{\iota}\kappa\eta$ is presented as a principle regarding the life of an individual as well as that of the society. the next stage of the development of this term will be an internalized principle of human behaviour.

BIBLIOGRAPHY*

Texts, Translations and Commentaries:

Thesaurus Linguae Graecae, A Digital Library of Greek Literature, CD Rom edition, University of California, Irvine

Homer, *The Iliad,* with an English translation by A.T. Murray, LOEB Classical Library, Cambridge-Massachusetts-London, vol. I-II, 1957

Homer, *The Odyssey,* with an English translation by A.T. Murray, revised by G.E. Dimock, LOEB Classical Library, vol. I-II, Cambridge-Massachusetts-London 1995

Homer, *Iliada,* przeł. K. Jeżewska, BN/II/17, Wrocław-Warszawa-Kraków-Gdańsk-Łódź 1986

Homer, *Iliada,* przeł. I. Wieniewski, Kraków 1984

Homer, *Odyseja,* przeł. L. Siemieński, BN/II/21, Wrocław 1953

Homer, *The Iliad, A Commentary,* edited by G.S. Kirk, Cambridge 1985

A Commentary on Homer's Odyssey, edited by A. Heubeck, Oxford 1988-92

Hesiod, *The Homeric Hymns and Homerica*, with an English translation by H.G. Evelyn-White, M.A., LOEB Classical Library, Cambridge-Massachusetts 1959

Hesiod, *Theogony,* edited with Prolegomena and Commentary by M.L. West, Oxford 1971

Hesiod, *Works and Days,* edited with Prolegomena and Commentary by M.L. West, Oxford 1982

Hezjod, *Narodziny bogów (Theogonia), Prace i dni, Tarcza,* przełożył J. Łanowski, Warszawa 1999

Elegy and Iambus with the Anacreontea, with an English translation by J.M. Edmonds, LOEB Classical Library, Cambridge-Massachusetts-Harvard 1954

Liryka Starożytnej Grecji, opr. J. Danielewicz, BN/II/ 97, Wrocław-Warszawa-Kraków-Gdańsk-Łódź 1987

Liryka grecka, wybór tekstów i komentarz, praca zbiorowa pod red. Jerzego Danielewicza: Tom I: *Jamb i elegia,* opr. K. Bartol, Tom II: *Melika,* opr. J. Danielewicz, Warszawa-Poznań 1999

---

* This bibliography comprises not only the works quoted in the survey, but also other books and articles that may be useful for the subject.

Adkins, A. W. H., *Values, goals, and emotions in the Iliad*, Classical Philology 77 (1982), 292-326

Poetic Craft in the early Greek Elegists, Chicago and London 1985

From the Many to the One, London 1970

Art, Values and Beliefs in the Last Book of the "Iliad", Classical Philology 80 (1975), 239-254

Merit and Responsibility, A Study in Greek Values, Clarendon Press 1960

Homeric Ethics, in: *A New Companion to Homer*, edited by I. Morris and B. Powell, Leiden-New York- Köln 1997, 695-713

The Greek Polis, Chicago 1986

Moral Values and Political Behaviour in Ancient Greece, London 1972

Arnheim, M. T. W., *Aristocracy in Greek Society*, Plymouth 1977

Balme M., *Attitudes to Work and Leisure in Ancient Greece*, Greece &Rome

Bartol K., *Liryka grecka, T. II, Jamb i elegia*, in: *Liryka Grecka, Wybór tekstów i komentarz*, praca zbiorowa pod red. J. Danielewicza, Warszawa-Poznań 1999

Bennet J., *Homer and the Bronze Age*, in: *A New Companion to Homer*, edited by I. Morris and B. Powell, Leiden-New York- Köln 1997, 511-534

Benveniste E., *Le vocabulaire des insitutions indo-europeennes*, Paris 1969

Barker E., *Greek Political Theory*, London 1977

Benardete S., *The Rhetoric of Morality and Philosophy*, Chicago-London 1995

Bowra C.M., *Heldendichtung. Eine vergleichende Phänomenologie der heroischen Poesie aller Völker und Zeiten*, Stuttgart 1964

Burchfiel K.J., *The Myth of Prelaw in Early Greece*, Symposion edited by G. Thür, 1993, 79-104

Cairnes L.D., *Aidos. The Psychology and Ethics of Honour and Shame in Ancient Greek Literature*, Oxford 1993

Bowra C.M., *Homer*, Duchwork 1972

Calhoun G.M., *The Homeric Picture*, in: *A Companion to Homer; Polity and Society*, edited by A.J.B. Wace and F.K. Stubbings, New York-1963, 431-452

Calhoun G.M., *Introduction to Greek Legal Science*, Oxford 1944

The Cambridge History of Literary Criticism, vol. I, edited by G. A. Kennedy

Cantarella E., *Spunti di reflessione critica su ΥΒΡΙΣ e ΤΙΜΗ in Omero*, Symposion 1978, 85-96

Chantraine P., *Dictionnaire éthymologique de la langue grecque*, Paris 1990

A Commentary on Homer's Odyssey, edited by A. Heubeck, Oxford 1988-92

Connor W.R., *The HISTOR in History*, in: *Nomodeiktes. Greek Studies in Honour of Martin Ostwald*, edited by R.M. Rosen and J. Farell, Michigan 1993, 3-15

Cornford F.M., *The Unwritten philosophy and Other Essays*, Cambridge 1967

Danielewicz J., *Morfologia hymnu antycznego. Na materiale greckich zbiorów hymnicznych*, Poznań 1976

Modlitwa i hymn w greckiej teorii i praktyce literackiej, in: M. Swoboda, J. Danielewicz, *Modlitwa i hymn w poezji rzymskiej*, Poznań 1981

Liryka starożytnej Grecji, BN II/92, Wrocław-Warszawa-Kraków-Gdańsk-Łódź 1987

Liryka starożytnej Grecji, Warszawa -Poznań 1996

Liryka Grecka, t. II, Melika, in: *Liryka Grecka, Wybór tekstów i komentarz*, praca zbiorowa pod red. J. Danielewicza, Warszawa-Poznań 1999

Darcus Sullivan S., *Psychological Activity in Homer. A Study of phren*, Ottawa 1988

Dembińska-Siury D., *Człowiek odkrywa człowieka. O początkach greckiej refleksji moralnej*, Warszawa 1991

Deneen P.J., *The Odyssey of Political Theory*, in: *Justice vs Law in Greek Political Thought*, edited by L.G. Rubin, Maryland 1997, 83-109

Detienne M., *Homere, Hesiode et Pythagoras*, Bruxelles-Bercheim 1962

Diamond A.S., *The History and Origin of Language*, New York 1965
Primitive Law Past and Present, London 1971
The Evolution of Law and Order, Westport-Connecticut 1975

Dickie A., *Dike as a Moral Term in Homer and Hesiod*, Classical Philology 73, 91-101

Dickinson G.C., *The Greek View of Life*, London 1962

Dihle A., *Der Begriff des NOMOS in der griechischen Philosophie*, in: *Nomos und Gesetz*, heraugegeben von O. Behrends und W. Sellert, Göttingen 1995, 17-134

Diller H., *Hesiod und die Anfänge der griechischen Philosophie*, Antike und Abendland, B. II (1946), 140-151

Dodds E.R.., *The Greeks and the Irrational*, Boston 1951

Donlan W., *The Aristocratic ideal in Ancient Greece*, Colorado Press 1980

Dworkin R., *Taking rights Seriously*, Cambridge Mass. 1977

Effenterre von, H. & M., *Arbitrages Homériques*, Symposion 1993, 3-10

Ehrenberg V., *Die Rechtsidee in frühen Griechentum*, Leipzig 1921
From Solon to Socrates. Greek History and Civilization during the Sixth and Fifth Centuries B.C., London 1968,
Polis und Imperium, edited by K.F. Stroheker and A.J. Graham, Zurich 1965 *The Greek State*, Oxford 1960

Eliade M., *Historia wierzeń i idei religijnych,* t. I, Warszawa 1988

Ephraim D., *Solon, Neutrality and Partisan Literature of late Fifth-century Athens,* Museum Helveticum 41 (1984), fasc. 3, 129-138

Erffa von, C., *Aidos und Vervandte Begriffe,* Philologus, suppl. 30, Leipzig 1937

Feske, Marthus, Reinhard, Rosen, *Geschichte der Politischen Ideen von Homer bis zur Gegenwert,* Königstein 1981

Finley M.I., *The World of Odysseus,* London 1956

Fraenkel H., *Early Greek Poetry and Philosophy,* Oxford 1965
Die Homerischen Gleichnisse, Göttingen 1971

Frame D., *The Myth of Return in Early Greek Epic,* Yale-New Haven-London 1978

Fritz von, K., *Totalitarismus und Demokratie im Allen Griechenland und Rom,* Antike und Abendland, B. VIII (1959), 47-74

Furley D.J., Allen R.E., *Studies in Presocratic Philosophy* (...), London 1970

Gagarin M., *Dike in the Works and Days,* Classical Philology 68 (1973), 81-94
Dike in Archaic Greek Thought, Classical Philology 69 (1974),
Oaths and Oath-challanges in Greek Law, Symposion 1995, 125-134
Early Greek Law, Berkeley-Los Angeles-London 1986
Morality in Homer, Classical Philology 82 (1987), 285-306

Gajda J., *Teorie wartości w filozofii przedplatońskiej,* Wrocław 1992

Gehrke H.J., *Der Nomosbegriff der Polis,* in: *Nomos und Gesetz,* heraugegben von O. Behrends und W. Sellert, Göttingen 1995, 13-35

Gernet L., *The Anthropology of Ancient Greece,* London 1981

Glotz G., *La cité grecque,* Paris 1988

Gould T., *The Ancient Quarrel between Poetry and Philosophy,* New Jersey 1991

Gschnitzer F., *Zur Normenhierarchie im öffentlichen Recht der Griechen,* Symposion 1979, 143-164

Guthrie W.C.K., *A History of Greek Philosophy,* Cambridge 1975-78

Hammond M., *City-State and World-State,* Cambridge 1954

Hart H.L.A., *Recht und Moral. Drei Aufsätze,* Göttingen 1971

Havelock E.A., *The Greek Concept of Justice,* Cambridge 1978
The Literate Revolution in Greece and Its Cultural Consequences, Princeton-New Jersey 1982
Dikaiosyne: An Essay in Greek Intellectual History, Phoenix 23 (1969)

Hirzel R., *Themis, Dike und Verwandtes,* Hildesheim 1966
Agraphos Nomos, Hildesheim 1979, 14-31
Der Eid, Aalen 1966

Hoffman W., *Die Polis bei Homer,* in: *Zur griechischen Staatskunde,* herausgegeben von F. Gschnitzer, Darmstadt 1969, 123-138

Hölscher U., *Heraklit zwischen Traditionen und Aufklärung,* Antike und Abendland B. XXXI (1985), 1-24

Hommel H., *Wahrheit und Gerechtigkeit,* Antike und Abendland B. XV (1969), 159-175
Solon, Staatsmann und Dichter, in: *Symbola, B. I, Kleine Schriften zur Literatur- und Kulturgeschichte der Antike,* heraugegeben von B. Gladiger, Hildesheim-New York 1976, 23-42

Die Gerichtsszene auf dem Schild des Achilleus. Zur Pflege des Rechts in Homerischer Zeit, in: *Symbola,* B. II, Hildesheim-Zürich-New York 1988 46-82

Horrocks G., *Homer's Dialect,* in: *A New Companion to Homer,* edited by I. Morris and B. Powell, Leiden-New York- Köln 1997, 193-217

Humphreys S.C., *Anthropology and the Greeks,* London 1978

The Iliad: A Commentary, edited by G.S. Kirk, Cambridge 1985

Irani K.D., *The Idea of Social Justice in the Ancient World,* in: *Social Justice in the Ancient World,* edited by K.D. Irani and M. Silver, Westport 1995, 3-8

Irwin T., *Classical Thought,* in: *A History of Western Philosophy I,* Oxford 1989 *Isonomia. Studien zur Gleiheitsvorstellungen im griechischen Denken,* herausgegeben von J. Mall und E.G. Schmidt, Berlin 1964

Jaeger W., *Paideia,* Warszawa 1968

Janszen N., *The Divine Comedy of Homer. Defining Political Virtue through Comic Descriptions of the Gods,* in: *Justice vs Law in Greek Political Thought,* edited by L.G. Rubin, Maryland 1997

Jones J.W., *The Law and Legal Theory of the Greeks. An Introduction,* Aalen 1977

Kagan D., *The Great Dialogue. History of Greek Political Thought from Homer to Polybius,* London 1965

Kennedy G., *Classical Rhetoric and Its Christian and seculr Tradition from Ancient to Modern Times,* North Carolina 1989

The Art of Persuasion in Greece, Princeton 1963

Kennedy G.A., *The Language and Meaning in Archaic and Classical Greece,* in: *The Cambridge History of Literary Criticism,* vol. I, edited by G.A. Kennedy, Cambridge 1989, 78-91

Kirkwood G.M., *Early Greek Monody. The History of a Poetic Type,* Ithaka-London 1974

Komornicka A.M., *Poezja starożytnej Grecji. Wybrane gatunki literackie,* Łódź 1987

Kornatowski W., *Rozwój pojęć o państwie w starożytnej Grecji,* Warszawa 1950
Zarys dziejów myśli politycznej starożytności, Warszawa 1968
Korus K., *Die griechische Satire. Die theoretischen Grundlagen und ihre Anwendung auf Homers Epik,* Kraków 1991
Nauka i nauczanie w opinii starożytnych Greków, Kraków 1980
Krokiewicz W., *Zarys filozofii greckiej od Talesa do Platona,* Warszawa 1971
Moralność Homera i etyka Hezjoda, Warszawa 1959
Kullmann W., *Antike Vorstufen des modernen Begriffs des Naturgesetz,* in: *Nomos und Gesetz,* heraugegeben von O. Behrends und W. Sellert, Göttingen 1995, 36-111
Larsen O., *Ethik und Demokratie,* 1990
Latte K., *Der Rechtsgedanke in archaischen Griechen,* Antike und Abendland B. III (1946), 63-76
Themis und Verwandtes, in: *Kleine Schriften;* herausgegeben von O. Gigon, W. Buchwald und W. Kunkel, München 1968, 141-145
Thesmos und Verwandtes in: *Kleine Schriften;* herausgegeben von O. Gigon, W. Buchwald und W. Kunkel, München 1968, 147-151
Lengauer W., *Polis i jednostka. Uwagi o kryzysie klasycznej politei,* Meander 32 (1977), 73-84
Pojęcie równości w greckich koncepcjach politycznych, Warszawa 1988
Lloyd G.E.R., *Polarity and Analogy,* cambridge 1966
Lloyd-Jones H., *Justice of Zeus,* Berkeley-Los Angeles-London 1971
Ehre und Schande in der griechischen Kultur, Antike und Abendland B. XXXIII (1987), 1-28
Lyons J., *Structural Semantics,* Oxford 1972
Łanowski J., *Hezjod. Narodziny bogów (Teogonia), Prace i dni, Tarcza,* Warszawa 1999
Manville P.B., *The Origins of Citizenship in Ancient Athens,* New Jersey 1990
Manteuffel J., *O demokracji ateńskiej,* Meander 1 (1946), 369-380
Mehmel F., *Homer und die Griechen,* Antike und Abendland B. IV (1954), 16-41
Machiavelli und die Antike, Antike und Abendland B. III (1948), 152-186
Morris I., *Homer and the Iron Age,* in: *A New Companion to Homer,* edited by I. Morris and B. Powell, Leiden-New York- Kööln 1997, 535-559
Mulroy D., *Early Greek Lyric Poetry,* The University of of Michigan Press 1992

Nagy G., *Images of Justice in Early Greek Poetry*, in: *Social Justice in the Ancient World*, edited by K.D. Irani and M. Silver, Westport 1995, 61-68

Nelson S., *Justice and Farming in the Works and Days*, in: *The Greeks and Us*, *Essays in Honour of A. W. H. Adkins*, edited by Louden-Schollmeier, 1996

Neschke A.B., Βουληφόρος ἀνήρ - *zur Bedeutung der sogenannten Diapeira im 2. Buch der Ilias (B, 1-483)*, Antike und Abendland B. XXXI (1985), 25-34

Nestle W., *Griechische Geistesgeschichte*, Stuttgart 1944

Vom Mythos zum Logos. Die Selbsentfaltung des griechischen Denkens, Stuttgart 1975

Ostwald M., *Autonomia. Its Genesis and early History*, Chicago 1982

Nomos and the Beginning of the Athenian Democracy, Oxford 1969

Page D., *The Homeric Odyssey*, Oxford 1955

Parnicki-Pudełko S., *Agora. Geneza i rozwój rynku greckiego*, Warszawa-Wrocław 1957

Pearson L., *Popular Ethics in Ancient Greece*, Stanford 1962

Peradotto J., *Modern Theoretical Approaches to Homer*, in: *A New Companion to Homer*, edited by I. Morris and B. Powell, Leiden-New York-Köln 1997,

Piper Handbuch der Politischen Ideen, herausegegeben von I. Fetscher und T. Meinkler, München- Zürich 1998

Podbielski H., *Mit kosmogoniczny w Teogonii Hezjoda*, Lublin 1978

Popper K., *An Open Society and Its Enemies*, Princeton 1971

Primmer A., *Homerische Gerichtszenen*, Wiener Studien 83 (1970), 5-13

Quass F., *Nomos und Psephisma*, Zetemata, München 1971

Raaflaub K.A., *Homeric society*, in: *A New Companion to Homer*, edited by I. Morris and B. Powell, Leiden-New York- Köln 1997, 380-395

Die Anfänge des politischen Denkens dei den Griechen, in: *Piper Handbuch der Politischen Ideen*, herausegegeben von I. Fetscher und T. Meinkler, München- Zürich 1998, 189-225

Roberts S., *Ordnung und Konflikt*, Stuttgart 1981

Robinson R., *Essays in Greek Philosophy*, Oxford 1969

Rodgers V.A., *Some Thoughts on DIKH*, Classical Quarterly 21 (1971), 289-301

Romilly de, J., *Pourquoi la Grèce?*, Paris 1992

Patiance, mon coeur. L'essor de la psychologie dans la littérature grecque des origines à Aristote, Paris 1971

Problemes de la démocratie grecque, Paris 1991

Rosen K., *Griechenland und Rom,* in: Feske, Marthus, Reinhard, Rosen, *Geschichte der Politischen Ideen von Homer bis zur Gegenwert,* Königstein 1981, 15-117

Rosen M.R., *Homer and Hesiod,* in: *A New Companion to Homer,* edited by I. Morris and B. Powell, Leiden-New York- Köln 1997,

Rosen S., *The Quarrel between Philosophy and Poetry. Studies in Ancient Thought,* Routledge 1988

Ruschenbusch E., *Die Polis und das Recht,* Symposion 1979, 305-326

Scully S., *Homer and the sacred City,* Ithaka-London 1990

Searle J.R., *Speech Acts,* Cambridge 1969

Snell B., *Poetry and Society,* Bloomington 1961

The Discovery of the Mind. The Greek Origins of European Thought, Oxford 1953

Stransburger H., *Die Einzelne und die Gemeinschaft im Denken der Griechen,* in: *Zur griechischen Staatskunde,* herausgegeben von F. Gschnitzer, Darmstadt 1969, 97-121

Tatarkiewicz W., *Historia filozofii,* Warszawa 1986

Tandy D.W., Neal W.C., *Hesiod's Works and Days. A translation and Commentary for the Social Sciences,* Berkeley-Los Angeles-London 1996

Thür G., *Oaths and Dispute Settlement in Ancient Greek Law,* in: *Greek Law in Its Political Settings,* edited by L. Foxhall and A.D.E. Lewis, Oxford 1996, 57-72

Turasiewicz R., *Życie polityczne w Atenach w V i IV w. p.n.e. w krytycznej ocenie współczesnych autorów ateńskich,* Wrocław-Warszawa-Kraków, 1968;

Demokracja ateńska a kwestia tolerancji światopoglądowej, Meander 46 (1991), 269-285

Wokół pojęcia thesmos, Meander 28 (1973), 379-384

W kręgu znaczeniowym pojęcia nomos, Meander 29 (1974), 7-22

Przeciwnicy swobód demokratycznych w Atenach IV w. p.n.e., Meander 21 (1966), 3-14

Wokół ateńskiej idei praworządności, Meander 22 (1967), 505-516

Polityczne oblicze literatury greckiej w V w. p.n.e., Meander 41 (1986), 357-374

Homer i jego świat, Kraków 1971

Studia nad pojęciem "kalos kagathos", Warszawa-Kraków 1980

Turner F.M., *The Homeric Question,* in: *A New Companion to Homer,* edited by I. Morris and B. Powell, Leiden-New York- Köln 1997,

Vatai F.L., *Intelectuals and Politics in the Greek World,* London-Sidney-Door-New Hampshire 1981

Vlastos G., *Studies in Greek Philosophy,* Princeton 1996

Vogt E., *Nitzsche und Wettkampf Homers,* Antike und Abendland B. XI (1962), 103-114

Webster T.L .B., *Die mykenische Vogeschichte der griechischen Drama,* Antike und Abendland B. VIII (1959), 7-14

Historical Commentary, in: *A Companion to Homer, Polity and Society,* edited by A.J.B. Wace and F.N. Stubbings, New York 1963, 452-462

Wesel U., *Geschichte des Rechts von Frühformen bis zum Verttrag von Maastricht,* München 1997

Whitman C.H., *Homer and the Heroic Tradition,* Harvard 1958

Wiliams B., *Shame and Necessity,* Oxford 1993

Witkowski S., *Państwo greckie. Historia ustroju państw greckich i obraz ustroju Aten i Sparty,* Warszawa 1930

Wolf E., *Griechisches Rechtsdenken,* B. I, Frankfurt am Main 1950

Wolff E., *Hegel und die griechische Welt,* Antike und Abendland B. I (1945), 163-181

Wolff H.J., *The Origin of Judical Litigation among the Greeks,* Traditio 4 (1946), 31-87

Zum Problem der dogmatischen erfassung des altgriechischen Recht, Symposion 1979, 9-20

Wood E., Wood N, *Class Ideology & Ancient Political Theory,* Oxford 1978

Wundt M., *Geschichte der griechischen Ethik,* Leipzig 1908

Wyganowski P., *Dike u Homera,* Meander 49 (1994), 327-340